Pyrrhus of Epirus

The tale of a King, Warrior and Philosopher of Ancient Greece

Hourglass History

Copyright © 2023 Hourglass History. All rights reserved.

No part of this publication may be reproduced, stored in a retrieval system, or transmitted in any form or by any means, electronic, mechanical, photocopying, recording, or otherwise, without written permission of the publisher.

Table of Contents

Chapter 1: The Enigma of Pyrrhus 1

Chapter 2: Birth of a King 5

Chapter 3: The Mountain Kingdom of Epirus 9

Chapter 4: Young Pyrrhus: The Exile 13

Chapter 5: Glorious Macedonia: A New Home 17

Chapter 6: The Silver Shadows: Life Under the Successors 21

Chapter 7: Rise to Power: The Return to Epirus 26

Chapter 8: Pyrrhus, the Philosopher King 40

Chapter 9: The Expansion Begins: War with the Molossians 47

Chapter 10: Master of the Adriatic 52

Chapter 11: The Call of Italy 56

Chapter 12: Pyrrhic Victories: The Italian Campaign 60

Chapter 13: Gods and Omens: Religion and Myth in Pyrrhus' Life 71

Chapter 14: A Clash with Carthage: The Sicilian Campaign 76

Chapter 15: Kingdom of the Sun: The Battle for Syracuse 82

Chapter 16: The Tides of Fortune: The Return to Italy 87

Chapter 17: ....92Benevolent Despot or Tyrant? Assessing Pyrrhus' Rule 92

Chapter 18: Warrior King: Pyrrhus at War...................97

Chapter 19: Pyrrhus and the Hellenistic World 102

Chapter 20: The Return to Epirus and the War with Macedonia 107

Chapter 21: Strained Alliances: Pyrrhus and the Aetolian League..112

Chapter 22: The Twilight Years: Pyrrhus' Later Reign 116

Chapter 23: The Fatal Rooftop: The Death of Pyrrhus 122

Chapter 24: Successors and Failures: Epirus After Pyrrhus 127

Chapter 25: A Look at Pyrrhus Through the Eyes of Historians 132

Chapter 26: Myths, Legends, and Folklore of Pyrrhus 137

Chapter 27: The Legacy of Pyrrhus in Modern Culture 141

Chapter 28: Pyrrhus and Rome: A Relationship Revisited..146

Chapter 29: The Lessons of Pyrrhus 150

Chapter 30: The Hourglass of Pyrrhus.......................155

Your Voice, Our Beacon..160

CHAPTER 1:

The Enigma of Pyrrhus

The image of Pyrrhus of Epirus in the annals of history is akin to a sphinx riddle—both intriguing and enigmatic. He flickers on the edge of historical illumination, lingering in the boundary zone where legends blur into fact, in the periphery of grand narratives dominated by figures like Alexander the Great and Julius Caesar. His tale unfolds, not with the thunderous proclamation of an emperor, but with the subtle intensity of an ever-burning flame—fierce, enduring, and paradoxically illuminating.

Pyrrhus was a son of Epirus, a child conceived in the mountainous bosom of Northwestern Greece, where the cypress and pine-draped landscapes whispered tales of ancient times, and rugged warriors etched their legends onto the face of history. His saga may have begun amidst the verdant slopes and tranquil valleys of Epirus, yet it swiftly spilled over the confines of his homeland, echoing through the expanses of the Hellenistic world.

In the grand theatre of history, Pyrrhus emerges as a figure of fascinating contradiction. His bloodline marked him for kingship, yet the capricious whims of fate dictated a formative period in exile. He learned early that power was a double-edged sword, glinting with promise on one side, and shadowed by betrayal on the other. He was hailed as an epitome of Hellenistic martial valor, his name often uttered in the same breath as Alexander the Great and Hannibal, and yet the victories he procured bore a cost so steep that they became synonymous with the term 'Pyrrhic victory'.

A philosopher-king in his own right, Pyrrhus contemplated the mysteries of power and governance, yet he himself often teetered on the precipice of reckless ambition. It's as if he stood at the intersection of a crossroad where the paths of wisdom and audacity crossed, creating a whirlwind of action and thought, victory and loss, endurance, and fatality.

A study of Pyrrhus's life is not merely an exploration of an individual's journey; it's an inquiry into the very heart of the Hellenistic age. He was a man of his times, reflecting the world he was born into—a world pulsating with the vibrancy of Hellenistic culture and reeling under the disarray following Alexander's death. His life was a complex tapestry of diplomatic maneuvering, martial exploits, and philosophical musings, all set against a backdrop of a time fraught with a volatile mix of possibilities and uncertainties.

Pyrrhus inhabited a realm of ceaseless turmoil, a period characterized by the constant oscillation of power dynamics, where the stage was shared by warriors and philosophers alike. This Hellenistic age bore witness to the grandeur of imperial aspirations, the carnage of relentless warfare, and the subtle intrigues of political machinations. Pyrrhus not only navigated this intricate maze of a world but left an indelible mark upon it.

The pursuit to unravel the enigma of Pyrrhus is an odyssey that transcends the boundaries of time and space. From the craggy heights of Epirus, through the opulence of Macedonian courts, across the windswept waves of the Adriatic to the golden shores of Italy and Sicily, and then back home—each landscape echoes a different facet of his life, each battle a testament to his undying spirit, each decision a reflection of his philosophy.

Who then, was Pyrrhus? Can he be confined to the labels history often doles out? Was he a hero, striding across the corridors of time with unquenchable valor? Or a ruthless adventurer, blinded by the intoxicating allure of power? Perhaps a visionary, who glimpsed a future others failed to perceive? Or was he a tyrant, his rule leaving bitter memories in its wake? As we delve into his life, we realize that Pyrrhus was a fusion of all these roles and more. He was a puzzle, the pieces of which were as complex and nuanced as the era he belonged to.

Pyrrhus of Epirus, the enigmatic King, the fearless warrior, the reflective philosopher, invites us on a journey—a journey back into a time when the world was in flux, where old norms were challenged, and new empires were dreamt of. A voyage into his life is a pilgrimage through the past, where echoes of ancient tales reverberate the tales of valor, wisdom, ambition, and the relentless quest for glory.

The story of Pyrrhus beckons us, promising a voyage across the turbulent seas of time, through lands soaked in history, to the heart of an enigma that continues to captivate the human spirit. A King, a Warrior, a Philosopher; Pyrrhus was all this and more, an intricate tapestry of contradictions and paradoxes, an enigma that tantalizes us across the millennia. Embark on this journey and step into the world of Pyrrhus, into the epic tale of a man who shaped the course of history in ways as multifaceted as the man himself.

CHAPTER 2:

Birth of a King

In the annals of time, when the veil of mystery hung low over the Hellenistic world, a child was born in the mountainous kingdom of Epirus, heralding a new epoch in the tapestry of history. It was here, amidst the rugged landscape adorned by the Cypress and Pine, where the murmuring waters of the Acheron river whispered tales of heroism and wisdom, that the young Pyrrhus began his saga. This son of Aeacides and Phthia was destined for an extraordinary life, though the course of that life, like the meandering streams of the Acheron, was as unpredictable as it was tumultuous.

The blood that coursed through Pyrrhus's veins bore the royal seal of the Aeacid dynasty, the lineage reputed to be descended from the mighty Achilles himself. The echoes of Achilles' glory reverberated through the young prince's upbringing, whispering tales of unparalleled heroism and complex humanity. Such tales were to Pyrrhus both an ancestral lullaby and a clarion call to greatness, a paradox that would remain with him throughout his life.

Born into a kingdom nestled amidst towering peaks and fertile valleys, Pyrrhus was cradled by the rugged landscape of Epirus. The towering mountains etched against the clear azure of the Greek sky were not merely a geographical feature to him; they were part of his identity. These grand guardians stood as silent sentinels throughout his formative years, shaping him with their untamed beauty and rugged resilience, lessons that the young prince absorbed like the roots of the age-old pines drank from the heart of Epirus.

As the young prince began to navigate his world, the echoes of the past guided his steps. The tales of Achilles' valor, Odysseus' cunning, and Hector's nobility danced before his eyes, as alive as the burning hearth in the royal hall. His tutors, wise scholars from the farthest corners of the Hellenistic world, imparted lessons that were as diverse as they were enlightening. Young Pyrrhus devoured knowledge with an insatiable hunger, be it the art of statecraft from the wise Epirote elders or the nuances of strategy from his father's seasoned generals.

Pyrrhus, much like the heroes of the ancient epics, exhibited signs of his future greatness from an early age. From his first steps, there was an assuredness, a certain clarity of purpose, that set him apart. He was a child marked by an intense curiosity, a desire to understand the world around him, and an uncommon level of determination. He questioned, he explored, and he learned, his mind expanding with each passing day, absorbing the knowledge and experiences that would shape the king he was to become.

Yet, the heart of this future king was not just filled with the pragmatism of statecraft and the cunning of warfare. In the quiet solitude of the Epirote nights, under the vast expanse of the star-studded sky, young Pyrrhus would lose himself in the tales of old, the exploits of the gods and the tragedies of heroes. These stories, steeped in the wisdom of generations, were not merely sources of entertainment for him. They were the threads that wove the tapestry of his imagination, shaping his understanding of honor, courage, and ambition. They were the bedrock of the moral compass that guided him, a beacon that illuminated his path even in the darkest of times.

The young prince, however, was not solely a creature of his royal court. Pyrrhus, much like his land, was an embodiment of contrasts. If the court symbolized the grace and sophistication of royalty, then the untamed wilderness of Epirus represented the raw vitality of life. The young prince was as comfortable amidst the rugged wilderness as he was in the gilded halls of his palace. He learned to ride before most children learned to walk, the sight of the young prince atop his horse, his laughter echoing through the valleys, was a testament to his indefatigable spirit.

However, young Pyrrhus' life was not all hero's tales and childhood adventures. The shadow of his destiny, foretold in omens and prophecies, hung over him from an early age. The oracles had spoken of his extraordinary future, of a life that would shape the course of history. The weight of these prophesies lay heavily on the young prince's shoulders, a constant reminder of the path that had been ordained for him. It was a path that would lead him through the heart of the Hellenistic world, a journey marked by victories, losses, and the ceaseless pursuit of glory.

The narrative of Pyrrhus' early life serves as a testament to the complexities of the human experience, to the intricate dance between destiny and choice, power and vulnerability, glory and sacrifice. The birth of this king was not merely an event; it was the dawn of an era that would shape the course of history. Amidst the rugged landscapes of Epirus, in the quiet solitude of the royal halls, a young prince was being prepared for his extraordinary destiny. And as Pyrrhus grew, so did the shadow he was to cast upon the world.

CHAPTER 3:

The Mountain Kingdom of Epirus

In the annals of history, place and character are intricately intertwined, each breathing life into the other's story. So it was for the child who would become Pyrrhus, King of Epirus, born into a world carved by the teeth of geological time and the sword of human ambition.

Epirus, where our young prince first opened his eyes to the world, is a realm of high drama. Its geography is a theatre of stark contrasts, a landscape where soft whispers of verdant valleys contend with the clamour of majestic mountains. The land ascends from the azure Ionian Sea into the Pindus Mountains' stony heart, peaks like the hands of giants reaching for the heavens, then descends into mist-filled valleys and river-cut plains.

Yet this stage was not merely a passive backdrop to Pyrrhus' life; it was an active participant. The harsh, rugged terrain mirrored the tenacious, unyielding spirit of the Epirote people - and of Pyrrhus himself. Here, the mountains were not just obstacles to be overcome but refuges to be cherished. In these impenetrable heights, communities found a fortress, a sanctuary against the constant threat of invasion. Thus, each stone, each boulder, became a bulwark of security in a turbulent world.

Equally significant was Epirus' position on the world's stage. Set on the periphery of the Hellenistic world, it was a gateway, a bridge between the western reaches of the Greek domain and the tribal territories of Illyria and Macedonia. This liminality conferred upon Epirus, and its future king, a unique position - part of the Hellenistic sphere, yet set apart.

Epirus was not Athens, nor was it Sparta. This was a kingdom built upon the convergence of cultures, a melting pot stirred by the currents of the Adriatic and Ionian Seas. The Epirotes held a special reverence for Zeus and the oracle at Dodona, thought to be the oldest in Greece, was situated here, a place where the gods whispered through the rustling leaves of sacred oak trees.

Yet, the realm of Epirus was not bound by the shimmering confines of myths alone; it was a place where reality carved the pathways of life as sharply as the tales told by firelight. Epirus was blessed with natural wealth, its resources a bountiful offering from the land. The rivers flowing through Epirus were not merely ribbons of life but veins of silver and gold. Copper and iron also lay hidden within the land's bosom, resources that could be transformed into tools, weapons, wealth.

The wealth of Epirus, however, was not solely mineral. Its people were a treasure in their own right. The Molossians, Chaonians, and Thesprotians - the main tribes that made up the Epirote league - were hardy folk, their spirits as unyielding as the mountains they called home. Though they spoke a dialect of Greek and worshipped the Greek gods, these tribes maintained a distinct identity, a sense of otherness.

The family into which Pyrrhus was born was of the Molossian tribe, the most powerful in Epirus, claiming descent from the mythical hero Achilles. This was a people whose lifeblood was the art of war, the rhythm of battle as familiar to them as the seasons. From an early age, boys were taught to fight and to ride, to master the spear and the sword. A boy born to rule them, then, would need to know more than just the weight of a crown; he would need to understand the heft of a sword, the balance of a spear.

The Epirotes, though, were not just warriors but herders and farmers. Despite the mountainous terrain, they coaxed life from the land, growing barley, oats, and vegetables, and tending to their flocks of sheep and goats. Thus, the future king would also need to know the rhythm of the seasons, the whisper of seeds growing into crops, the lowing of cattle, and the bleating of sheep.

Epirus, this cradle of mountain and sea, was more than the place of Pyrrhus' birth. It was the crucible of his making. The lessons he learned here - the rhythm of the seasons and of battle, the language of diplomacy and war, the weight of a sword and a crown - these were the building blocks of the man he would become.

The young prince was born to Aeacides and Phthia, a coupling that wove him into the grand tapestry of myth and power, for his parents were said to descend from none other than Achilles, the greatest of Greek warriors, and Andromache, the loyal wife of the Trojan hero Hector. Pyrrhus, thus, inherited a lineage steeped in courage, resilience, and, inevitably, tragedy.

Such was the world into which Pyrrhus was born - a world of rugged mountains and whispering gods, of warrior tribes and bountiful land. From this multifaceted tapestry of place and culture, Pyrrhus, the King, the Warrior, the Philosopher, took his first steps on the path of destiny. His journey, like the landscape of his homeland, promised to be one of stark contrasts and dramatic moments, a voyage shaped by the inexorable tide of history and the indomitable spirit of the man himself.

CHAPTER 4:

Young Pyrrhus: The Exile

To grasp the fate of young Pyrrhus, we must summon forth the inexorable specter of time, allowing it to sweep us back into the maelstrom of political struggle, treachery, and conflict that was the cradle of the young prince's exile. It is here, within this crucible of power and intrigue, that we discover how an ousted boy of royal lineage began to mould himself into a figure of legend.

Our tale begins in the Epirote court, a stage set for a brutal contest of power and succession. Pyrrhus, a child of but two years, the fledgling offspring of King Aeacides and Phthia, a descendant of the renowned Aeacidae lineage, found himself at the epicenter of this perilous storm. The shadow of his father's contentious reign and eventual dethroning by the opposing faction loomed ominously over his infant life, poisoning the wellspring of his childhood with the bitter draught of exile. In the year 317 BC, Pyrrhus, accompanied by his guardians, was thrust out of the royal palace and into the rugged Epirote landscape, the first bitter taste of his nomadic journey.

With their homeland now a forbidden terrain, Pyrrhus and his guardians sought refuge within the welcoming arms of their Illyrian neighbors. Bardylis, the chieftain of the Dardanian Kingdom, would prove to be their benefactor. A potentate who himself knew the stinging realities of power struggles and territorial conflicts, Bardylis would come to play a central role in shaping Pyrrhus' formative years. His court, vibrating with the constant hum of warfare and political manoeuvring, was a world-class institution of realpolitik.

It was here, under Bardylis' watchful gaze, that Pyrrhus was to receive his first lessons in the arts of survival, the delicate balance between diplomacy and warfare, and the ever-present specter of treachery. Far from an ideal childhood, Pyrrhus found himself in a crucible, where his character was tested, tempered, and ultimately, forged. Pyrrhus, the child, was being refashioned into Pyrrhus, the king-in-waiting.

The political intrigue that wove itself around Pyrrhus was not merely a background echo to his formative years. In truth, the young prince was the linchpin of these machinations, a nascent symbol of power and hope to those who had been loyal to his father. As the threads of intrigue were pulled and stretched across the region, Pyrrhus became the living embodiment of a cause - the reclaiming of Epirus from its usurpers, the restoration of the Aeacidae dynasty, the rising phoenix that so many were banking on.

Yet, the intensity of the political machinations that ensnared him was to have profound effects on Pyrrhus. It necessitated a maturity and steeliness far beyond his tender years. It also imbued him with a sense of purpose and resolve, a fire that would remain an integral part of his character throughout his life.

However, it was not merely the broader, more political aspects of his exile that shaped him. Just as vital were the personal trials and tribulations, the individual losses and triumphs. The young prince, forced to grapple with his displacement, was exposed to the harsh realities of the world far sooner than most. From an early age, Pyrrhus was to understand that life was fraught with uncertainty, that security and stability were but fleeting moments in the ebb and flow of existence.

Amid these challenges, however, Pyrrhus also learned valuable lessons about loyalty, friendship, and trust. He discovered that alliances could be fickle, often as fleeting as autumn leaves in the gusting wind, but that true loyalty, once earned, could prove to be as enduring as the mighty oaks of the Epirote landscape. These were lessons that would serve him well in the years to come.

As Pyrrhus matured, the indelible marks of his early exile began to manifest themselves in his demeanor and conduct. There was a restless energy about him, an insatiable hunger for power and dominance. These were traits that, no doubt, had their roots in his turbulent childhood. Yet, they were also colored by his experiences in Bardylis' court and his growing understanding of the complex dance of power.

Yet, despite the trauma of his early exile, there was no sense of resentment or bitterness within the young prince. Instead, what emerged was a robust, resilient character with a keen understanding of the political landscape and the will to shape it to his advantage.

In essence, the exile of Pyrrhus was a catalyst, a crucible in which the prince was refashioned into a king. Far from breaking him, the harsh realities of his early years forged him into a formidable force. His saga was a testament to the enduring power of resilience and the indomitable spirit of an individual who, despite the odds, managed to rise above his circumstances and etch his name in the annals of history.

And so, the stage was set for Pyrrhus' journey from a young prince in exile to the towering figure of history we know today. In the maelstrom of political struggle and personal challenges, the boy was being shaped into the man, the displaced prince was being forged into the king, the casualty of power was being transformed into its master.

CHAPTER 5:

Glorious Macedonia: A New Home

In the canvas of human history, the childhood of great men often seems to be painted with the brushes of hardship and tribulation. Such was the case with Pyrrhus. Born into royalty yet catapulted into exile, he grew amidst tumultuous power plays that inevitably sculpted the king, warrior, and philosopher he was to become. This chapter illuminates the turn of events that spirited Pyrrhus away from the stark confines of Illyrian exile towards the vibrant heart of Macedonia.

Our tale begins in the rugged landscapes of Illyria, where young Pyrrhus, a scion of Epirote royalty, found refuge in the court of King Glaukias. An ambitious figure of tumultuous character, Glaukias held sway over the Illyrian Kingdom nestled between the grandeur of Macedonia and the Adriatic's azure expanse. In this frontier, where civilization met wilderness, Glaukias thrived, wielding influence and power in equal measure.

Glaukias' position on the throne was not unchallenged, however. Bardylis, the renowned Illyrian chieftain, remained a formidable presence, casting a long shadow over the Illyrian political landscape. A warrior-king of considerable prowess, Bardylis had been a thorn in the side of Macedonia, felling kings and battling armies. His relations with Glaukias were complex, a labyrinth of political maneuvering, alliances, and rivalry. Yet, it was under this delicate power balance that Pyrrhus found refuge, and the intricate dance of Illyrian politics became his early education.

However, the wheel of fortune was always turning. Bardylis' death – a momentous event that disrupted the status quo – provided an unexpected opportunity for the young Pyrrhus. With Bardylis gone, the threat to Macedonia from the Illyrian front diminished considerably, and a gap emerged in the regional power dynamics.

No longer was Pyrrhus destined to remain ensconced in the Illyrian hills. Instead, he found himself called to the opulence of Macedonia, the land of Alexander the Great. The young exile, now merely twelve, was plucked from the harsh Illyrian terrain and introduced to the heartland of Hellenistic power.

The transition was seismic. Suddenly, the rugged, mountainous Illyrian landscapes gave way to the vibrant cityscapes of Pella. Here was a city bustling with activity, an epicenter of Hellenistic culture and power, resonating with the legends of Alexander's grandeur. Yet, beneath its architectural splendor simmered the complex interplay of politics and power.

Amid these new surroundings, Pyrrhus was not a mere observer; he became an active participant in the labyrinthine political game of Macedonia. The lad who once roamed the rugged landscapes of Illyria now walked through the grand corridors of Pella, where the echoes of past glories met the murmurings of present intrigues.

His arrival in Macedonia signaled a metamorphosis. Guided by the seasoned hand of Antigonus Gonatas, Pyrrhus learned to navigate the treacherous currents of power politics. In the Macedonian court, lessons were learned not in the warmth of a teacher's lecture but amidst the frigid realities of political machinations. Yet, it was here that Pyrrhus began to hone his skills as a future leader, balancing strength with diplomacy, power with friendship.

Macedonia offered more than political instruction, though. It was here that Pyrrhus was exposed to the rich tapestry of Hellenistic culture. He traversed the colonnaded paths of Pella, engaged with the enlightened minds in the Agora, and absorbed the intellectual wealth of his age. It was an education as much cultural as it was political, shaping not just a king, but a philosopher.

By the time Pyrrhus' chapter in Macedonia closed, he had evolved beyond the wide-eyed boy of Illyria. He had matured into a leader, a thinker, a budding warrior. His experiences had etched indelible marks on his character, infusing him with a keen understanding of power, culture, and war.

Macedonia was more than a sanctuary for Pyrrhus. It was a crucible where he was tested, a stage where he began to come into his own, and a springboard that would propel him towards future challenges. Pyrrhus departed Macedonia carrying more than just memories. He bore the lessons and experiences that would shape his destiny, forming the foundation of the extraordinary life that awaited him. As we trace his footsteps through the annals of history, we realize that Macedonia was not merely a chapter in his life. It was the prologue to a saga of heroism, ambition, and philosophical thought that would echo through time.

CHAPTER 6:

The Silver Shadows: Life Under the Successors

In the wake of the great Alexander's death, the Hellenistic world slipped into an era of volatile flux, a period defined by tectonic shifts in power, grand alliances, treacherous betrayals, and monumental battles. This was the era of the Diadochi, the Successors, Alexander's generals, who tore at the edges of his empire like ravenous wolves.

This was the world into which Pyrrhus was thrust, a world caught in the shadow of towering figures and their ceaseless power struggles. This was no place for the weak, the indecisive, or the naïve. It was a merciless crucible that tested mettle, wit, and ambition. But even as the tumult of this era swirled around him, Pyrrhus was not simply tossed in the tempest. He was a vessel, charting his course through the storm, learning, adapting, evolving.

The Successors were larger than life figures, men whose ambitions extended beyond the mortal realm. Each sought to carve out a piece of Alexander's empire for himself, their lofty dreams rivaled only by the depths of their ruthlessness. Amidst this pantheon of warriors and strategists, Pyrrhus learned the invaluable lesson that power and survival hinged on shrewd political maneuvering and an adaptable war doctrine.

Pyrrhus's early days in the court of Antigonus Gonatas, the sturdy ruler of Macedonia, were transformative. He learned that the art of war was not confined to battlefields; it unfolded in the grand halls of power, whispered in the corridors of influence. It was a chess game of alliances and betrayals, promises and threats, where a word could be as lethal as a sword.

His exposure to the Successors' war games was not a passive observation; it was a masterclass in strategy. He studied their moves, their decisions, their victories, and their defeats. Each battle waged, each city besieged, each peace treaty signed, etched indelible marks on Pyrrhus's understanding of power and war. His time in the Macedonian court was a crucible that forged his political and military acumen.

But the Successors were more than mere power players. They were the bearers of Alexander's legacy. In their ambition, their relentless pursuit of power, they embodied the spirit of their late conqueror. In them, Pyrrhus glimpsed the reflection of Alexander's indomitable spirit. He saw men who dreamt beyond the horizon, who dared to challenge the gods themselves in their quest for glory. From them, Pyrrhus gleaned that to be a king, to rule, was to dream, to dare, and to conquer.

The shadows of the Successors loomed large over Pyrrhus, not as daunting specters, but as luminous constellations illuminating his path. He absorbed their wisdom, imbibed their courage, mirrored their ambition, but he was not a mere reflection. He was his own light, kindling the fire of his destiny, casting his own shadow.

For Pyrrhus, the Successors were not just bearers of power; they were the epitome of Hellenistic artistry in warfare. He learned from them the harmony of force and finesse, the symphony of strategy and strength. Each Successor, in his way, demonstrated the art of command, the cadence of leadership, the rhythm of rule.

Antigonus, with his resilient spirit and unfaltering courage, epitomized the steadfastness of leadership. Cassander, the ruler of Macedonia, was a living testament to the efficacy of cunning and pragmatism. Lysimachus of Thrace exemplified the might of patience, and Ptolemy, the satrap of Egypt, personified the power of intellect.

Each of these giants offered a unique perspective, a distinctive approach to power, war, and rule. They were the individual notes that composed the grand symphony of Hellenistic leadership. And Pyrrhus was there, in the heart of this grand spectacle, absorbing every note, every nuance.

In these men, Pyrrhus saw not just rulers, but also men. Men of flesh and bone, desire and fear, strength and weakness. He saw their greatness, their flaws, their triumphs, and their failures. And in these realizations, he found reflections of his own self, his own aspirations, his own fears. The Successors, for all their might and wisdom, were mortal, just as he was. They bled, they faltered, they doubted, just as he did.

But they also dreamed, they dared, they fought, they conquered, and so would he. Pyrrhus was not destined to merely stand in their shadows; he was destined to cast his own. He was not born to merely follow their paths; he was born to chart his own. For Pyrrhus, the Successors were not the end; they were the means, the steppingstones on his journey towards greatness.

The world of the Successors was a crucible that molded Pyrrhus, an anvil on which his character, his spirit, his ambition were forged. They were the silver shadows that cast light on his path, illuminating the rugged landscape of power, war, and kingship.

Yet, Pyrrhus was not their echo; he was his own voice. He was not their shadow; he was his own substance. He did not dwell in their twilight; he kindled his dawn. For, in the grand theater of the Successors, Pyrrhus was not a mere spectator; he was an actor, a player, a king in the making.

Thus, in the arena of the Successors, amid the thunderous clashes of ambition and power, Pyrrhus learned, adapted, and grew. He transformed from a young, exiled prince into a budding leader, a promising strategist, a discerning king. Forged in the crucible of the Successors' world, Pyrrhus emerged as a figure of resilience, ambition, and wisdom, ready to carve his name in the annals of history.

And so, the Silver Shadows served not as his shackles, but as his wings. They were not his ending, but his beginning. For Pyrrhus, they were the dawn that heralded the arrival of his day, the day of Pyrrhus, the King, the Warrior, and the Philosopher.

CHAPTER 7:

Rise to Power: The Return to Epirus

Return of the Prodigal Son

If one casts an eye over the shimmering landscape of ancient Epirus, where towering mountains mingle with the verdant green of the valleys, one can begin to discern the rhythm of a drama unfolding. A young king, as much a pariah as he was a hero, had returned. But this was not just any return; it was the homecoming of Pyrrhus, the exiled king. The prodigal son of Epirus was back, and he bore a gleam in his eyes that spoke of both ambition and resolve.

But first, one must delve into the circumstances of this homecoming. Pyrrhus' return to Epirus was more a resolute stride than a hesitant step. In his heart simmered a potent blend of ambition and determination, tempered by the cold lessons of his exile. His claim to the throne of Epirus, once taken from him by the tendrils of conspiracy and intrigue, now served as a beacon, guiding him through the rough waves of political opposition.

As he sailed across the Ionian sea, Epirus might have appeared a rough diamond to him, but it was a diamond nonetheless. He knew its value, the lush valleys that could feed an army, the high mountain passes offering natural defenses, the loyalty of its people to their true king. And so, armed with the knowledge of its worth and driven by his vision, he began his ascent, an ascent that was to be as challenging as the mountainous terrain of his homeland.

When Pyrrhus set foot on Epirote soil once again, he did not arrive as a conquering outsider, but as one of their own. His blood was their blood, his history, their history. But could the son of Aeacides, barely more than a child when he was torn from his throne, convince the Epirotes to rally behind him? He began with a small band of followers, faithful companions and allies he had won during his exile, men who believed in him, not just the king, but the man behind the crown.

In his bid to raise an army, Pyrrhus did not lean solely on these loyalists. He reached out to the local Epirotes, who had suffered under the rule of the usurper Neoptolemus. Their hearts yearned for justice and peace, for a ruler who was one of them. Pyrrhus, a victim of the same injustice that had fallen upon them, was the answer. His charisma, honed in the courts of the Diadochi, drew them to his cause.

Yet, raising an army from the Epirote populace was not without its challenges. The Epirotes, predominantly composed of fierce tribal groups, were as divided as they were united in their defiance of Neoptolemus. But Pyrrhus understood that their loyalty would not be won merely by blood ties or shared grievances. He knew that he had to give them something to believe in, a cause, a vision. And so, he offered them the dream of a united Epirus, strong and free under a just king. It was an ideal that ignited the flame of hope in their hearts and spurred them to rally under his banner.

But Pyrrhus' burgeoning force was not solely comprised of Epirotes. He was a pupil of the Diadochi, and he had learned from them the value of a diverse army. To the pool of Epirote warriors, he added mercenaries attracted by promises of wealth and land. These were battle-hardened men, skilled in the art of war and loyal to the coin. It was a precarious balance, this army of his. The local Epirotes and foreign mercenaries, driven by different motives, could have easily turned on each other or on him. But Pyrrhus held them together. He was their fulcrum, their common ground.

One must wonder, though, at how a man not yet in his thirties could command such a diverse force. The answer lay in Pyrrhus' charisma and his understanding of what drove these men. To the Epirotes, he was the rightful king, the son of Aeacides, returning to reclaim his birthright. To the mercenaries, he was a ticket to wealth, a king who valued their skills and was willing to pay for them. Each man saw in Pyrrhus a leader who understood him and valued him, and that was a compelling reason to follow.

In the nascent period of his return, the composition of Pyrrhus' force was a reflection of his own multifaceted identity. It was as much Epirote as it was Macedonian, as loyal to the vision of a united Epirus as it was to the gold that awaited them at the end of the campaign. Pyrrhus' army was not just a military force; it was a symbol of his vision for Epirus. And as they began their march towards destiny, one could almost sense the stirrings of history in their footsteps.

The army of Pyrrhus was, in many ways, a mirror image of the man himself. Like him, it was a blend of diverse elements – the rugged, home-grown strength of Epirus, the cold efficacy of foreign mercenaries, the loyalists won over by the man Pyrrhus had become during his years of exile. It was a motley crowd, but there was a sense of purpose in their stride, a fervor in their eyes that spoke of their faith in the man leading them. Pyrrhus had become a beacon of hope, an embodiment of the ambition that lay within each Epirote heart.

Yet, the army that Pyrrhus had raised was not just a symbol; it was a potent force. It was an army built not just on lofty ideals, but also on the pragmatic realities of warfare. It was a force composed of varying elements, each lending its strength to the whole. The Epirotes provided the bulk of the infantry, their familiarity with the local terrain proving a considerable advantage. The mercenaries, with their diverse backgrounds, brought with them a variety of fighting styles, adding an element of unpredictability to Pyrrhus' force.

The size of the army, too, was a reflection of Pyrrhus' ambition. While exact numbers are lost in the mists of time, accounts suggest that it was an army of considerable size, enough to challenge Neoptolemus and his cohorts. Yet, it was not the size of the army that mattered as much as the way Pyrrhus utilized it.

Pyrrhus understood the value of each element in his army and used them to their full potential. He did not just throw them into battle; he applied them with precision, like a sculptor chipping away at marble. The Epirote infantry formed the solid core of his force, their knowledge of the terrain and their personal vendetta against Neoptolemus making them a formidable adversary. The mercenaries, meanwhile, were his wild card. They were deployed where they were needed most, their unpredictability and their skill keeping Neoptolemus on his toes.

But it was not just Pyrrhus' strategic acumen that made his army effective. It was also the bond that he had forged with his men. To them, he was not just their king; he was their comrade, their leader. He understood their needs, their hopes, their fears. He did not just command them; he inspired them. It was this bond, more than any strategic acumen, that transformed his diverse force into an effective, cohesive unit.

Thus, as Pyrrhus embarked on his campaign to reclaim his throne, he did not march alone. He had with him an army, not of faceless soldiers, but of men who believed in him, who were ready to fight for him. The prodigal son of Epirus had returned, not as a helpless victim of circumstance, but as a king, a leader, a beacon of hope. And as he stood on the threshold of reclaiming his throne, one can imagine the gleam in his eyes, the fire in his heart. The stage was set for the next act of his grand drama, and Pyrrhus was ready to play his part. For he was not just the prodigal son of Epirus; he was its hope, its future, its king.

A War for Hearts and Minds

In the canvas of history, battles do not merely stand as violent encounters between opposing forces; they are also potent symbols, a display of power and strategy that can inspire as much as they can intimidate. As Pyrrhus prepared to wage war against Neoptolemus, he was not simply launching a military campaign; he was embarking on a war for hearts and minds.

Pyrrhus was no stranger to the battlefields. He had seen wars, fought in them, and learned from the best, the successors of Alexander the Great. And he had not merely learned to fight; he had learned to wage a war strategically. But as he set foot on the battlefield as the leader of his own army, one can imagine the weight of responsibility that bore down on him, for he was not merely fighting for himself, but for the people of Epirus, for their hopes and dreams.

The early clashes between Pyrrhus and Neoptolemus were a testament to this approach. Each battle was a careful calculation, an intricate dance of power and strategy where each move was not only aimed at vanquishing the enemy but also at sending a message. Pyrrhus' strategy was not just about winning battles; it was about winning hearts.

Each skirmish, each clash of steel, was a performance designed to inspire. He was the underdog, the true king challenging the usurper. Every victory, no matter how small, was a potent symbol of his commitment, his determination, his ability to lead. And as word of these victories spread, so did his reputation. The people saw in Pyrrhus a leader, a warrior, a king who could stand up to Neoptolemus, and they rallied to his cause.

But Pyrrhus knew that inspiring his people was only half the battle won. The other half lay in his own troops. After all, they were the ones who had to fight, to put their lives on the line. And so, he turned his attention to them, seeking to win their hearts just as he had won the hearts of his people.

Each victory, each display of his strategic acumen, served to inspire his troops, to bolster their faith in him. But Pyrrhus went beyond just inspiring them. He connected with them, understood their needs and concerns, and addressed them. He treated them not as mere pawns in his grand game, but as individuals with their own hopes and fears. This understanding, this connection, endeared him to his troops and forged a bond of loyalty and trust that would stand the test of time.

Yet, the road to the throne was not smooth. Despite the victories, the momentum, the growing support, Pyrrhus knew that his biggest challenge lay ahead - the decisive face-off against Neoptolemus. It was a battle that would not only determine his fate but the fate of Epirus itself.

As Pyrrhus prepared for this decisive confrontation, one can only imagine the whirlwind of thoughts in his mind. He was on the cusp of reclaiming his throne, but the final hurdle was the hardest. Yet, he was not alone in his struggle. He had with him an army that believed in him, that was ready to fight for him. And as he stood before them, not just as their king but as their comrade, one can sense the bond of trust and loyalty that held them together.

The final battle against Neoptolemus was a spectacle of strategy and bravery. Pyrrhus, despite the odds, commanded his forces with a calm and determined demeanor. He used his knowledge of the local terrain to his advantage, deploying his Epirote warriors in key positions, utilizing the unpredictability of his mercenaries to confuse the enemy. Each move was a testament to his strategic acumen, a lesson learned from the Diadochi brought to life on the battlefield.

And his men fought with a fervor that matched their leader's. They fought for their king, for their homeland, for the promise of a better future. And as the dust settled, they emerged victorious, not just over Neoptolemus, but over the shadows of their past.

The defeat of Neoptolemus was a turning point for Pyrrhus. It was more than just a military victory; it was a triumph of his vision, his leadership. He had promised his people a better future, and he had delivered. And as word of his victory spread, his reputation grew. He was no longer just the rightful king of Epirus; he was the hero who had defeated the usurper, the leader who had brought hope to a beleaguered people.

Pyrrhus used these victories to strengthen his position, to solidify his power. He reached out to the local population, promising justice and peace. He worked tirelessly to win their trust, to build a bond that was based on shared dreams and ambitions. And as he stood before his people, not just as a victorious king but as a humble servant, one can sense the respect, the admiration, the love that they held for him.

But even as he basked in the warmth of his victory, Pyrrhus did not forget his soldiers. He rewarded them for their bravery, acknowledging their contribution to his victory. He treated them not just as his troops but as his comrades, his brothers-in-arms. This approach, this connection with his soldiers, served to further strengthen the bond between them. They had fought for him, risked their lives for him, and they saw in Pyrrhus a king who valued their sacrifice, who understood their struggles. And this understanding, this bond, would prove crucial in the challenges that lay ahead.

As Pyrrhus stood triumphant, one can almost sense the change in the air, the shift in the tides. He had returned to Epirus as an exiled king, but he had claimed his throne not as a conqueror, but as a liberator, a servant of the people. He had won not just the throne, but the hearts and minds of his people. And as he looked towards the future, one can imagine the gleam in his eyes, the resolve in his heart. For he was not just the king of Epirus; he was its beacon of hope, its symbol of resistance, its hero. And as the curtain fell on this chapter of his life, one could only wonder at the heights he would reach, the history he would write, in the chapters to come.

The King's Justice and a Warrior's Ambition

It is one thing to win a throne, quite another to sit on it and rule justly. As Pyrrhus stood victorious, the crown back on his head, he was not merely the king of Epirus; he was its hope, its promise for a brighter future. And with this hope came an enormous responsibility – the need to rule wisely, justly, and for the benefit of his people.

Pyrrhus was no stranger to the machinations of politics and power. But ruling was different from waging war. It required a delicate balance of force and persuasion, of ruling with an iron fist and yet maintaining a velvet touch. And Pyrrhus knew that he had to tread this path carefully, for the wounds inflicted by Neoptolemus' rule were still raw.

From the onset, Pyrrhus' rule was marked by his commitment to justice. It was not the draconian justice meted out by a tyrant, but the balanced, compassionate justice of a ruler who valued the welfare of his people above all else. His initial reforms were aimed at unifying the fragmented Epirus, at healing the wounds that the strife had inflicted.

He set about reforming the laws, removing the imbalances that had existed. He sought to address the grievances of the common people, often overruling the powerful aristocracy. Pyrrhus knew that the true strength of a kingdom lay in the happiness of its people, and he did his utmost to ensure their well-being. He created an atmosphere of trust and loyalty, of shared dreams and ambitions, a place where every Epirote, regardless of his social standing, felt that they mattered.

But while he sought to rule with benevolence, Pyrrhus was no pushover. He understood that to maintain order, to ensure the rule of law, he needed to exhibit firmness. He did not shy away from meting out justice where it was warranted, showing his people that while he was their king, he was also the upholder of justice, the one who would ensure that the rule of law prevailed.

Yet, even as Pyrrhus worked towards securing his rule and healing his land, the warrior in him was restless. The fire that had ignited in him when he first held a sword, the desire to carve his name in the annals of history, still burned bright. Epirus was his home, but he knew that his destiny lay beyond its borders. And so, he turned his gaze to the larger Hellenistic world, to the ripe fields that awaited his conquest.

Pyrrhus knew that to fulfill his ambitions, he needed an army – not just any army, but a force that could match his ambitions, that could stand toe to toe with the best that the Hellenistic world had to offer. He began to transform the small, mixed force that had helped him reclaim his throne into a formidable army. He trained his soldiers, taught them the tactics he had learned from the Diadochi, inculcated in them the spirit of the warrior. He bolstered the ranks with the best from Epirus, seasoned veterans and raw recruits, eager to make their mark.

The composition of Pyrrhus' army was a reflection of his understanding of warfare and his strategic acumen. He knew that while local Epirotes formed the backbone of his army, he also needed the skills and expertise that came with mercenaries, who brought with them experiences from different battlefields. This diversity gave Pyrrhus an edge, enabling him to adapt his strategies based on the battle and the enemy.

Pyrrhus was well aware that the size of his force was a vital factor. He had seen how large armies could tip the balance in favor during his time in Macedonia and amongst the Diadochi. Pyrrhus began to expand his army, attracting soldiers with the promise of glory and riches. By the time he was done, he had at his command a force that was a match for any in the Hellenistic world.

Yet, as he built his army, Pyrrhus never lost sight of his ultimate goal – his grand ambitions. He was not content with being just the King of Epirus; he desired to be a major player in the Hellenistic world, to etch his name in the sand of time. He dreamt of conquests, of expanding his realm, of making Epirus a force to be reckoned with.

As Pyrrhus stood surveying his land, his people, one could sense a calm before the storm. He had returned to Epirus as a prodigal son, reclaimed his throne, and brought about a reign of justice and prosperity. But the warrior in him yearned for more, for glory, for conquest. And as he set his sights on the world beyond Epirus, one could feel the winds of change, the stirring of a new chapter in the tale of Pyrrhus, the King of Epirus, the Soldier of Fortune, the Eagle of the North.

The stage was set, the pieces in place. The world waited with bated breath as Pyrrhus, the King of Epirus, prepared to unfurl his wings and soar. And as he looked towards the horizon, one could almost hear the distant rumble of thunder, the promise of the storm to come. But for now, there was a moment of calm, a moment to savor the peace before the storm, a moment to take a deep breath before plunging into the whirlwind of destiny.

For Pyrrhus knew, as he looked towards the future, that his journey was far from over. It was merely the beginning, the start of a saga that would reverberate through the annals of history. And as he prepared for the trials and tribulations that awaited him, one could only wonder at the heights he would scale, the challenges he would overcome, the history he would write, in the chapters to come.

CHAPTER 8:

Pyrrhus, the Philosopher King

When we recount the tale of Pyrrhus, we often evoke the image of a warrior, a ruler, a brilliant military strategist. Yet, to comprehend the enigma that was Pyrrhus, we must delve into another facet of his persona: Pyrrhus, the philosopher king.

The term philosopher king conjures a figure of contemplative disposition, ruling not by might, but guided by wisdom and a sense of justice. Pyrrhus might seem an unlikely candidate for this lofty title, his life often overshadowed by the noise of clashing swords and the clamor of conquest. Yet, beneath the layers of martial endeavor and political ambition, there lay a philosophy, a worldview, that infused his actions and illuminated his statecraft.

Pyrrhus' philosophy of kingship was neither chronicled in scholarly tomes nor immortalized in stately prose. It was articulated in his actions, the decisions he made, the way he wielded power, and how he envisioned his relationship with his people. He was a man of action, a king whose philosophy was the lived experience of his reign.

His rule in Epirus revealed a leader who was more than just a military commander. It showcased a man of vision, capable of seeing beyond the immediate demands of power and conflict, towards the longer-term considerations of governance and societal harmony. His efforts to heal the wounds inflicted by Neoptolemus' rule, his attempt to unify a fragmented Epirus, his pursuit of justice and order, all hint at a philosophical underpinning, a bedrock of values that guided his reign.

In Pyrrhus, we see echoes of the Aristotelian ideal of a king who is 'first among equals'. He saw himself not as a lofty monarch, detached from his subjects, but as part of the fabric of Epirus society. He was acutely aware of his duty to his people, not just as their king but also as their protector, their advocate. The concept of 'philanthropia', the love of humanity, seems to have been embedded in his approach to rule. Pyrrhus, it appears, understood that a king's legitimacy and longevity stemmed from the trust and loyalty of his people, won not just on the battlefield but also in the day-to-day governance of the realm.

Evidence of this understanding is visible in his reforms, marked by an egalitarian streak unusual for his time. His laws aimed at rectifying imbalances, addressing grievances, often going against the vested interests of the powerful aristocracy. Pyrrhus' philosophy saw no place for unjust privilege, his vision of a stable Epirus hinged on fairness, on the equal application of justice. He understood that for a society to flourish, it needed a foundation of equity, a sense of shared destiny, of communal harmony.

Pyrrhus, however, was not a utopian dreamer. He was a pragmatic philosopher, who recognized that ideals, while crucial, needed to be tempered with reality. He understood the complexities and contradictions of power, the necessity of wielding authority with firmness. His justice was compassionate, but when the situation demanded, it could also be stern, unyielding. He was a king who knew when to extend a hand of friendship and when to clench a fist of authority.

In Pyrrhus' dealings with his court and his subjects, we see a leader who valued counsel, who was not afraid to listen to opposing views. While his word was ultimately law, he created an atmosphere where discussion and debate were encouraged, not stifled. He knew that wisdom often came from the crowd, that a good king needed to be a good listener.

Yet, the philosophy of Pyrrhus was not confined to his internal governance alone. It extended to his dealings beyond the borders of Epirus, his approach to diplomacy and warfare. Pyrrhus, unlike some of his contemporaries, was not a reckless conqueror, a despot driven by a hunger for territories. He was a strategic thinker, who valued the diplomatic game as much as the military one.

His interventions were often guided by a larger vision, a calculated understanding of risks and rewards. He engaged with the world not merely as a king of Epirus but as a player in the Hellenistic world, acutely aware of the larger dynamics at play. He approached alliances and conflicts with a discerning eye, assessing not just the immediate gains but the long-term implications.

In this, Pyrrhus exhibited a certain Stoic understanding of the interconnectedness of events, of the ebb and flow of power. His philosophy of kingship extended beyond his own realm, into the shared space of the Hellenistic world. He was not an isolated figure, ruling over an isolated kingdom, but a part of a larger tapestry, aware of the intricate weave of relations that bound him to the world beyond Epirus.

In Pyrrhus, then, we find a philosopher king, albeit of a different mold. His philosophy was not enshrined in the quiet sanctum of a scholar's study but in the throbbing heart of the political arena. He was a king who thought deeply about his role, about the nature of power, and the responsibility it entailed. His philosophy was born not of abstract speculation but of concrete experience, tested and honed in the crucible of leadership.

In Pyrrhus, we find a fusion of thought and action, theory and practice, ideas, and their execution.It's a testament to his philosophical leanings that even in the throes of war, Pyrrhus often sought counsel from philosophers and scholars. He frequently invited intellectuals to his court, indulging in discourse that went beyond military stratagems and statecraft. His court in Epirus, like that of the Ptolemies in Alexandria, had the aroma of intellectual ferment, an undercurrent of lively debate and scholarly exchange.

The philosopher king of Epirus had a particular fondness for the teachings of Epicurus. Although a warrior to his core, Pyrrhus found merit in the Epicurean notion of 'ataraxia', the pursuit of tranquility and freedom from fear. While this might seem a contradiction, it's possible to interpret Pyrrhus' fondness for Epicureanism as his aspiration for inner peace amidst the tumult of war and politics. Could it be that Pyrrhus sought in philosophy what his turbulent life denied him? It's a tantalizing prospect that sheds new light on his complex persona.

In the end, perhaps the most profound expression of Pyrrhus' philosophy is found in his view of life and death. The tales speak of Pyrrhus' composure in the face of death, his acceptance of it as an inevitable part of life. One anecdote recounts how he once said, "The grave is the harbor of life." In this stoic acceptance of mortality, we see a glimpse of his philosophical leanings, a worldview that saw life and death as two sides of the same coin.

In the arena of power, where life was often a game of shadows and death a constant companion, Pyrrhus brought a unique philosophical perspective. He saw kingship not just as a right but as a duty, an opportunity to leave a lasting impact, to shape the course of history. He viewed the throne not as a seat of privilege but as a platform for change, for justice, for societal progress.

In this sense, Pyrrhus was indeed a philosopher king. His philosophy might not have been codified in scholarly treatises, but it was etched in the annals of his rule, in the hearts of his people, and in the unfolding narrative of Epirus. His philosophy of kingship was one of balance, balancing the demands of power with the pursuit of justice, balancing the needs of the state with the welfare of the people, balancing the rigors of war with the call for peace.

The story of Pyrrhus is not just a tale of a warrior, a king, or even a great military tactician. It is the story of a philosopher king who navigated the treacherous currents of power with wisdom and foresight. A king who, through his actions and decisions, infused his rule with a philosophy born of his experiences, his reflections, and his deep understanding of the human condition.

Pyrrhus' philosophy was a testament to his belief in the possibility of a better world, a world ruled by justice, tempered by compassion, and enriched by wisdom. It was a vision that guided his reign, inspiring his people, shaping his legacy, and cementing his place in the annals of history. Through his philosophy, Pyrrhus bestowed upon Epirus more than victories and territories; he bequeathed a legacy of thought, a blueprint of enlightened kingship, that resonates to this day.

In the mosaic of his life, the philosopher's stone is perhaps the most defining piece, providing a unique lens through which we can understand and appreciate the enigma that was Pyrrhus. In this king who ruled with the sword yet guided by wisdom, we find an embodiment of the philosopher king, a rare blend of thought and action, power and wisdom, that continues to captivate the imagination.

The tale of Pyrrhus, then, is not just the chronicle of a king but also the odyssey of a thinker, a visionary who sought to harmonize the practical demands of rule with the loftier ideals of justice and fairness. Through his rule, his life, and his legacy, Pyrrhus the philosopher king offers a lesson that remains as relevant today as it was in the tumultuous era of the Hellenistic world: that power, guided by wisdom, tempered by justice, and mindful of the common good, can be a force for lasting change.

In the corridors of time, the echo of Pyrrhus' philosophy still reverberates, reminding us of a king who dared to dream, a warrior who dared to think, a philosopher who dared to rule. It is in this enduring echo that we find the true legacy of Pyrrhus, the philosopher king of Epirus.

CHAPTER 9:

The Expansion Begins: War with the Molossians

When the winds of ambition began to rustle through the courts of Epirus, they did not sing a gentle song. They howled a cacophony of expansion, churning the otherwise calm political atmosphere of this mountain kingdom. It was as if the entire region, at the cusp of significant change, held its breath for the inevitable upheaval. And the man to herald this new age was none other than Pyrrhus, newly seated on his rightful throne.

Now king, the world was his to conquer. But before he could dream of reaching the shores of Italy or the deserts of Africa, there was a challenge that lay right at his doorstep. The neighboring Molossians, a tribe of proud and fiercely independent people, eyed his rise with both suspicion and defiance.

Pyrrhus was no stranger to the Molossians. He knew their mettle. These were the people of the highlands, hardy, resilient, molded by the rough and inhospitable terrain. Their land was rugged, the people tougher. Famed for their martial prowess, the Molossians were far from an easy conquest.

Why then, you might ask, would Pyrrhus pick such a formidable enemy for his first war of expansion? Was it hubris, fresh from his triumphant return to the throne? Or was it the reckless audacity of youth? No, dear reader. It was Pyrrhus, the tactician. He understood that before he could play in the grand chessboard of the Hellenistic world, he needed to consolidate his position at home. A war with the Molossians was not just a display of strength; it was a strategic necessity.

The war began with a clash of bronze and iron, the thunderous roars of men, and the neighing of horses. Pyrrhus led from the front, his scarlet cloak a vibrant splash of color amid the dust and chaos of the battlefield. His voice echoed across the field, a clarion call to his men. To those watching, he was a radiant figure, a beacon in the tumult, a sight to both inspire his troops and strike fear in the hearts of the Molossians.

There was a kind of wild poetry in the way Pyrrhus waged war. He was not just a king in armor, leading his men. He was the very embodiment of the warrior spirit, a storm of fury and determination unleashed. His courage was not silent or stoic; it was a roaring tempest, an all-consuming fire that spread through his ranks, setting alight the same fervor in the hearts of his men.

Yet, even in the thick of battle, there was a strange serenity about Pyrrhus. Amid the clash of arms, the cries of warriors, and the groans of the dying, Pyrrhus found a kind of peace. A strange calm, a sense of purpose that anchored him amidst the storm of war. He was, after all, not just a king, but a philosopher. And in the heart of this philosopher-king, war was not just about conquest, but also about understanding the limits of human endurance and the indomitable spirit of man.

The battles with the Molossians were fierce, the victories hard-won. But with each passing conflict, the strength of the Molossians waned, their resistance slowly but surely eroded by the relentless tide of Pyrrhus' forces. Their highland fortresses fell, one after the other, their warriors slain or captured, their lands annexed to the growing domain of Pyrrhus.

Yet, in his victory, Pyrrhus did not gloat. He did not let the thrill of conquest blind him. Instead, he showed magnanimity. The defeated Molossians were treated with respect. Their leaders were not humiliated but honored. Their warriors were not enslaved but integrated into his army. The Molossian lands were not pillaged but managed, their resources not exploited but used to fuel the development of Epirus.

In this, we see a glimpse of Pyrrhus, the statesman. His rule was not marked by the tyranny of the victor but characterized by a keen understanding of statecraft. He knew that to hold his newly expanded kingdom together, he needed not just to conquer lands but also win hearts.

Thus, in his early conquests, Pyrrhus laid down a blueprint for his future expansion: a combination of military prowess and political acumen, of courage in battle and magnanimity in victory, of personal valor and strategic foresight. It was this blend that would characterize his rule and his subsequent campaigns.

The war with the Molossians was more than just a territorial expansion for Pyrrhus. It was a testament to his philosophy of war and leadership. It showcased a king who was not just a warrior but also a thinker, not just a conqueror but also a statesman. It revealed a leader who understood the complexities of power, the intricate dance of war and politics, the delicate balance of fear and respect.

As Pyrrhus stood at the edge of the conquered Molossian lands, gazing out at the horizon, the Adriatic Sea shimmering in the distance, he knew he had passed the first test of his kingship. His war with the Molossians had been a gamble, a roll of the dice in the game of power. But Pyrrhus had played his hand well. He had proven his mettle, not just to his people, not just to his neighbors, but to the larger world that watched from the wings. He had shown that he was more than just a king; he was a force to be reckoned with.

So, it was that the tale of Pyrrhus, the conqueror, began. With the fall of the Molossian highlands, a new chapter in the history of Epirus was written. But this was just the beginning. More trials awaited Pyrrhus, more battles, more victories, and more losses. His destiny was not just to rule Epirus but to shape the course of history. And as he would soon discover, history, like the gods, is a fickle master.

CHAPTER 10:

Master of the Adriatic

On the weather-beaten shores of the Ionian sea, nestled amongst the multitude of Greek islands, sat a jewel so precious it became a much-contested prize throughout the annals of ancient history. It was the island of Corcyra, now known as Corfu. To those who held it, this pearl of the Adriatic served as a beacon of prosperity and prestige; it was a symbol of dominance over this vital sea trade route. The great Pyrrhus, already a proven conqueror on land, now cast his ambitious gaze towards the gleaming horizon of the Adriatic, seeking to add a naval mantle to his heroic array.

Our tale begins, as so many do, with an invitation. The Corcyraeans, embroiled in civil strife, had called for aid from Pyrrhus, to quell the dissension and reestablish order. The beleaguered islanders were aware of the Epirote king's reputation as a formidable military leader and hoped his involvement would tip the scales in their favor. From Pyrrhus' perspective, this was not just a plea for assistance, it was an opportunity, a gateway to greater influence and control in the region.

Corcyra's strategic location on the Adriatic's mouth made it a naval linchpin between the Hellenistic East and the increasingly ambitious states of the Italian peninsula. Control over the island meant controlling the trade routes, and consequently, a significant sway over the political dynamics in the region. Pyrrhus, ever the strategist, recognized this golden opportunity. Thus, he set forth on his Adriatic ambitions, with a fleet carrying the hopes of an empire.

His naval expedition to Corcyra was the first significant test of Pyrrhus' maritime acumen. Epirus, though wealthy in its rugged, mountainous terrain and warrior culture, lacked a strong naval tradition. To mount a successful sea campaign, Pyrrhus had to overcome not only the geographical challenges but also a deficiency in naval expertise among his men.

The call from Corcyra came not just with an opportunity but also with an implicit challenge: Could Pyrrhus of Epirus, the proven master of land battles, replicate his military success in the realm of Poseidon? If Pyrrhus intended to assert control over the Adriatic and thus extend his influence further into the Mediterranean world, he would need to answer this question affirmatively.

The answer, as we will see, was as complex as the man himself.

While the land welcomed the sure-footed Pyrrhus with familiar terrain and reliable tactics, the sea was an entirely different mistress. It required a unique set of skills and a level of adaptability that tested even the most seasoned of warriors. Pyrrhus, though not a natural seafarer, was never a man deterred by a challenge.

Assembling a fleet for his Adriatic campaign, Pyrrhus brought the same diligence and foresight that characterized his land campaigns. He drafted experienced seamen from the Ionian coast and sought the help of Demetrius the Besieger, his former ally and an experienced naval commander, for a share of his experienced fleet.

The fleet that Pyrrhus amassed was a potent mix of tactical innovation and seafaring tradition. He understood that the success of his naval expedition relied as much on the morale of his sailors as it did on the strength of his triremes. He nurtured a spirit of camaraderie and instilled in his seamen a sense of purpose, aligning them to his ambition.

The journey to Corcyra was fraught with the capricious nature of the sea. Yet, Pyrrhus, who led from the front, weathered the storm, both metaphorically and literally. The chronicler Dionysius of Halicarnassus recounts a tale of a violent tempest that beset Pyrrhus' fleet en route to Corcyra. It was here that Pyrrhus, the warrior king, added yet another layer to his legend.

In the face of the storm, while his men panicked, Pyrrhus stood unflinching on the deck of his ship, braving the rain and the raging sea. He seized the helm, navigating his vessel through the tumultuous waves, inspiring his men by his courage. By dawn, the storm had abated, and Pyrrhus, drenched and weary but unbowed, led his fleet into the safe harbor of Corcyra.

Upon landing, Pyrrhus wasted no time. His entrance into the city of Corcyra was one of calculated grandeur, designed to project the image of a savior. He brokered peace between the warring factions, uniting them under his banner.

Now, as the master of Corcyra, Pyrrhus stood as a notable naval force in the Adriatic. He had gained control of a significant strategic point and displayed his capacity to lead not just on land, but also on sea. The master of the Adriatic had secured his title.

As the ripples of his naval conquest spread across the region, Pyrrhus' reputation as a formidable power in both land and sea solidified. This naval victory would mark the beginning of a new chapter in Pyrrhus' career, one that highlighted his strategic flexibility and adaptability. His success at Corcyra was a testament to his unwavering determination, military genius, and his ability to mold himself according to the needs of the hour.

Pyrrhus of Epirus had become a dual threat, a king who could command both on land and sea. As the master of Corcyra, he held the reigns to the mouth of the Adriatic, and his eyes were set on greater horizons, his heart beat with the rhythm of the waves, eager for the next adventure that awaited him.

CHAPTER 11:

The Call of Italy

The great chessboard of the Mediterranean lay in a delicate state of flux in the late 3rd century BC, a vast network of city-states, tribal domains, and burgeoning empires entwined in a dance of power, prestige, and subtle antagonism. At the far western end of the Hellenic world, Italy was the theatre where destiny was preparing a new act for Pyrrhus of Epirus.

In that epic saga of the ancient world, the nature of the dance was such that the music could change abruptly, transforming a peaceful pavane into a violent tarantella. And so, in the year 280 BC, it did. From the Italian city of Tarentum, desperate and bellicose, a plea for help against Rome was cast across the Ionian Sea, landing squarely on the lap of Pyrrhus.

Tarentum was an anomaly in the rugged landscape of southern Italy, a relic of Magna Graecia, clinging obstinately to its cultural heritage amidst the rising tide of Roman expansion. Lavishly adorned with monuments and sculptures of exquisite beauty, its aristocrats reveled in a life of enlightened leisure, their hands ostensibly kept clean of the brutalities of war.

Despite its cultural grandeur, Tarentum found itself unable to mount a substantial defense against the burgeoning Roman force, a brawnier, more pragmatic breed of warrior. The Tarentines, ensconced in their enlightened city-state, were akin to silk-draped deer entrapped by the oncoming headlights of the Roman juggernaut. Their sophistication made them ill-equipped to meet the war machine that was Rome, yet, their pride forbade them to submit.

Why, you might wonder, did the call for help come to Pyrrhus, of all people? It is perhaps less surprising when one considers the intricate interplay of alliances, obligations, and political maneuverings of the Hellenic world. Pyrrhus, through his assertive reign, his considerable martial skill, and strategic acumen, had become a beacon of Hellenic power. His victories over the Molossians and his adept navigation of Adriatic politics had resonated across the Ionian Sea, reaching the anxious ears of Tarentum's elite. They sought a savior, a champion, a warrior-king who could halt the relentless Roman advance.

And Pyrrhus, eager to write his own destiny, answered the call.

It's crucial to underline that this decision wasn't the product of whimsy or a blind desire for glory. Pyrrhus was many things, but he was not a gambler. The meticulousness that had marked his campaign against the Molossians, the sharp foresight he had demonstrated in his naval expedition to the Adriatic, were the same traits he brought to bear on this new venture. Each possible outcome, each potential risk and reward, would have been carefully weighed in his mind before he made his decision.

Consider, if you will, the geographical positioning of Italy, its long peninsula a veritable bridge between East and West. For Pyrrhus, a foothold in Italy could serve as a launching pad for further ambitions, a platform from which he could assert his influence over the central Mediterranean, and even perhaps, one day, march upon Rome itself.

Yet, beyond the cold logic of strategy, there was also a more profound consideration at play, one that touched on the very essence of Pyrrhus' identity. He was, at his core, a man of the Hellenic world, a son of Zeus and Achilles in his own mind, born to defend the honor and prestige of Hellenic civilization. Tarentum's plea, therefore, was not simply a call for military aid. It was a cry for the preservation of the Hellenic way of life, a desperate appeal to stem the Latin tide.

There was, too, the allure of an honorable challenge. The reputation of the Romans had, by this time, grown considerably. They were no longer the awkward infantrymen of the early Republic, but a formidable force that had subjugated the Latin tribes and was pushing ever southwards, their gaze fixed firmly on the rich lands of Magna Graecia. To confront such an opponent was, for a man of Pyrrhus' temperament, irresistibly enticing. It promised not just territorial gains, but something far more valuable: everlasting glory.

And so, his mind resolved, Pyrrhus prepared his forces for the venture that lay ahead. He summoned his veterans, his hot-blooded Epirotes, his steadfast Macedonians, even the mercenary warriors who flocked to his banner. He inspected his phalanxes, his cavalry, his famed elephants, the living embodiments of his military prowess. Each soldier, each horse, each ponderous pachyderm, was not just a cog in Pyrrhus' war machine but a piece in the grand game that was about to be played out on the Italian stage.

Across the Ionian Sea, Tarentum awaited her champion. The dice of destiny had been thrown, and Pyrrhus of Epirus was sailing towards Italy, his sails filled not just with the winds of the sea, but with the breath of history, pushing him towards his date with destiny.

Thus, Pyrrhus answered the call of Italy. A chapter in his story was closing, another one was about to begin, one that would intertwine his fate with that of Rome, a clash of powers that would echo through the corridors of time. And the Mediterranean, that great stage of antiquity, waited with bated breath to witness the dance of the Epirote King and the Roman Wolf.

CHAPTER 12:

Pyrrhic Victories: The Italian Campaign

The Eve of Battle

On the precipice of the audacious journey, the king of Epirus, Pyrrhus, a seasoned warrior and burgeoning philosopher, was encased in contemplative solitude. The typically unwavering eyes that had stared down countless adversities now appeared to waver slightly. The approaching winds of the Adriatic Sea carried a distinct flavour of a daunting yet thrilling challenge that lay ahead. It was a strange mix of apprehension and anticipation. For as he stood on the rocky outcrops of his homeland, gazing into the moon-dappled expanse of water, Pyrrhus was not merely facing the prospect of a sea voyage. He was confronting the boundary of his known world. The vast sea was a formidable barrier, a chasm that separated him from the foreign land of Italy, pulsating with a tumultuous brew of conflict, intrigue, and potential glory.

Italy, a land in flux, was a patchwork of fiercely independent city-states. There, a diverse array of cultures and military traditions thrived. The Greek cities of Magna Graecia had become the southern bastion of Hellenistic civilization, each a shining jewel in its own right. They were veritable treasure troves of wisdom and power, each city a thriving center of commerce, culture, and military prowess. However, the very vibrancy of this environment was overshadowed by an existential threat. Rome, an insatiable beast of expansion, was gnawing at their freedom, seeking to homogenize their diversity under its dominion. Rome's ambition had set the stage for a confrontation that would go down in the annals of history, and at the center of this grand drama, was Pyrrhus, called to aid by his fellow Hellenes.

The mighty host of Epirus was a sight to behold. It was a carefully balanced blend of strength and agility, a formidable machine of war ready to unleash its wrath upon the adversaries. An impressive force of twenty thousand foot soldiers, three thousand horsemen, two thousand archers, and twenty war elephants comprised the army of Pyrrhus. The inclusion of war elephants was a distinctive stroke of military genius. These towering beasts, known but unseen by the Romans, would become harbingers of a new kind of warfare, a testament to Pyrrhus' audacious and innovative approach to battle.

Among the ranks of the soldiers and officers, there were also men from the Italian city-states, allies who had pinned their hopes on Pyrrhus' promised aid. Tarentum, in particular, a proud city teetering on the precipice of subjugation by Rome, had sent envoys to Epirus. The Tarentines, overwhelmed by the relentless Roman advance, had sought the aid of Pyrrhus. They were guided by a twofold sentiment: fear and hope.

Fear stemmed from the relentless march of Rome, a seemingly unstoppable force that threatened their way of life. Hope, on the other hand, was fuelled by the tales of Pyrrhus' bravery and tactical prowess.

The preparations for this vast campaign were a colossal task in themselves. The requirements of a large army, the supplies needed for a protracted war, the training required to maintain the sharpness of the troops, and the intricate plans needed to coordinate these myriad elements, it was a logistical nightmare. But, if anything, Pyrrhus was an excellent planner. His years in the Macedonian court, his previous military expeditions, and his encounters with the Successors of Alexander had sharpened his skills. He proved to be a strategic maestro, adept at foreseeing potential problems and making contingencies to overcome them.

However, even as the logistical machine worked at full throttle, Pyrrhus was acutely aware that this war was unlike any he had fought before. He was stepping into an unfamiliar landscape, fraught with unknown political dynamics. His success wouldn't merely depend on the outcomes on the battlefield but also on his ability to navigate the complex web of alliances and enmities among the Italian states. It was a high-stakes game with rules yet to be fully comprehended.

As the imminent battle approached, Pyrrhus of Epirus, the enigmatic king, soldier, and thinker, stood ready. His heart pounded to the rhythm of war drums, his mind buzzed with strategies, tactics, and contingencies. And yet, beneath all the noise, his soul was tranquil. He was about to step into an epic contest, and he was determined to play his part to the fullest.

As the first rays of dawn broke over the Adriatic, the stoic king didn't flinch. The day was here. The journey would soon begin. His moment of destiny was at hand. Italy awaited. The hour of the Pyrrhic victories was nigh.

The Italian Campaign

In the pregnant dawn of a new day, the warships of Epirus crested the indigo waves of the Adriatic. Their prows cut through the sea like a multitude of bronze beaks, bound for the sun-drenched shores of Italy. Pyrrhus, standing resolute on the deck of his command vessel, felt the breath of Thetis on his cheek as he peered into the horizon, the land of his destiny drawing ever closer. The chessboard of war had been laid, and the pieces were being meticulously positioned. This was not a war to be won solely by the strength of steel; this was a contest that required the precision of a weaver and the foresight of an oracle.

A storm of steel awaited Pyrrhus on the Italian soil. The Battle of Heraclea, his first contest against the indomitable Roman legions, would test his mettle in ways that he had not imagined. Rome's disciplined ranks, armed with their formidable pilum and gladius, stood arrayed like an impenetrable wall of iron. Against this stood the forces of Epirus, a multi-faceted array of

Greek hoplites, cavalry, and the wild card – elephants. It was here that Pyrrhus would introduce Rome to the sheer terror these beasts could inflict. They would lumber into battle, towers of flesh and tusk, striking fear into the Roman ranks. Pyrrhus, atop his steed, would guide this symphony of chaos and destruction, his keen eyes and tactical brilliance shaping the course of the battle.

The Battle of Heraclea was a grinding, bloody affair. Pyrrhus demonstrated a command of strategy and a personal bravery that resonated through the ranks. He plunged into the melee, his presence bolstering the resolve of his men, a paragon of kingly virtue in the thick of battle. His sword cut swathes through the enemy, his shouts of encouragement rallying his troops. Pyrrhus of Epirus was not a king content to observe from the rear; he was a warrior-king, the first into the fray, the last to retreat.

However, his victories did not come without cost. The Roman legions were a tough, relentless adversary, their discipline and courage matching that of the Greeks. Despite Pyrrhus' innovative tactics, the Roman infantry's tenacity led to heavy casualties on both sides. Pyrrhus' victories were akin to the tender kiss of a lover laced with venom, each one exacting a terrible price. The cost was not only in the lives of his men but also in the slow depletion of his resources and the erosion of his initial optimism.

The Battle of Asculum was a testament to this bitter truth. Pyrrhus and his army emerged victorious, but the victory was a crippling one. His forces were severely depleted, and the Italian allies looked upon these Pyrrhic victories with growing concern. Yet, in the face of such adversity, Pyrrhus proved to be more than just a great warrior; he showed himself to be a leader of men. He galvanized his troops, boosted their morale, and managed the delicate task of maintaining the alliance with the Italian city-states. He reassured his allies, managed their expectations, and addressed their fears. Pyrrhus, in his characteristic style, transformed the grim situation into a narrative of defiance and perseverance.

However, the relationship between Pyrrhus and his Italian allies was not without its complications. The Samnites, Lucanians, and the Bruttians had joined Pyrrhus out of a common fear of Roman aggression. Yet, their loyalty was contingent on Pyrrhus delivering swift and decisive victories. As the campaign progressed and the body count rose, tensions flared, and Pyrrhus found himself managing a complex network of alliances and expectations. However, his diplomatic acumen shone as brightly as his martial skills. Pyrrhus knew that to maintain the cohesion of his forces and keep the morale high, he needed to display an unwavering resolve, even in the face of growing adversity. He strove to maintain a delicate balance between encouraging his allies and pushing them for support, maintaining their trust and cooperation through the grueling campaign.

As Pyrrhus navigated through the treacherous terrain of military and political strategy, he faced not only the formidable power of Rome but also the fickle whims of his allies. Yet, his resilience in the face of adversity, his prowess on the battlefield, and his astute political mind shaped the campaign into a saga of Greek courage and ingenuity against the growing might of Rome. These Italian campaigns, fraught with victories that carried the sting of defeats, would forever associate the name Pyrrhus with the paradoxical phrase – a Pyrrhic victory. Yet, the campaign was more than just the sum of its battles; it was a testament to the spirit of a king who dared to challenge the formidable Roman Republic in its own backyard. Pyrrhus of Epirus, even in his victories laced with the poison of loss, would forever be remembered as a warrior who fought not for conquest, but for the freedom of the Greek cities in the face of Roman aggression. His campaign, while exhausting and costly, would forever be etched in the annals of history as a testament to audacity, courage, and the indomitable will of a king.

Reflections on Pyrrhic Victories

The smoke had barely dissipated when the last of the Roman footmen receded from the battlefield. The resounding silence bore witness to the ferocity of the clashes at Heraclea and Asculum, a terrifyingly vivid tableau of death and despair. Pyrrhus, astride his mount, surveyed the carnage with a sense of grim satisfaction mingled with deep sorrow. The cost of victory had indeed been high, the battlefield littered with the lifeless forms of his own men, a stark testament to the paradox of war. The Greek word 'nikē' meaning victory, seemed to ring hollow on the scorched plains of Southern Italy, the joy of triumph tainted by the bitter taste of loss.

In this strange limbo between success and catastrophe, Pyrrhus wrestled with the dichotomy of his victories. Each battle won had exacted a price that felt more like defeat than conquest. The king of Epirus had emerged victorious in the eyes of the world, but the cost rendered these victories Pyrrhic - a term that would, in the eons to come, bear his name and define the nature of such paradoxical successes.

In the immediate aftermath, it was not the cheer of victory that resonated through the encampments of Epirus, but the lament for the fallen. The toll was not just in lives, but also in the depletion of resources and the attrition of the allies' morale. Pyrrhus' victory felt like a wounded beast, triumphant yet scarred, and the weight of this duality bore heavily upon him.

The diplomatic fallout from the Pyrrhic victories was like a seismic wave that sent ripples through the political landscape of Italy. The Italian allies, who had once looked upon Pyrrhus with hopeful eyes, now beheld him with a mixture of respect and apprehension. The Samnites, Lucanians, Bruttians, and other Italian tribes, who had sought the protection of Pyrrhus against the burgeoning Roman aggression, now found themselves questioning the cost of their newfound freedom.

The victories, as costly as they were, had managed to check the Roman expansion momentarily. The strategic scales had tipped, albeit precariously, in favor of the Greeks and their allies. However, the aftermath of the campaign would lead to a renewed sense of urgency in Rome, eventually culminating in the consolidation of the Italian peninsula under Roman rule.

Pyrrhus' campaign was a double-edged sword, a shimmering beacon of Hellenistic resistance against Rome, and at the same time, a stark warning about the true cost of war. The phrase "Pyrrhic victory" was coined in the aftermath of this bloody campaign, forever symbolizing victories that inflict such a devastating toll on the victor that they equate to a loss. The concept found resonance in military and political contexts, a poignant reminder of the destructive potential of ambition, even in the pursuit of noble causes.

As the dust settled over the battlefields, the contemplative King of Epirus stood amidst the ruins of his victories, his heart weighed heavy with the realities of his success. Pyrrhus had journeyed to Italy as a champion of Hellenistic freedom, his spirit ablaze with dreams of crushing Roman supremacy. He had hoped to liberate the city-states of Magna Graecia from the clutches of Roman aggression, bolstering his ranks with allies united under the banner of liberty. He had landed on the Italian soil, not as a conqueror, but as a savior, a beacon of hope for the beleaguered city-states.

However, in the end, the victories won by Pyrrhus were both his crowning glory and his ultimate undoing. The steep price paid for each triumph had exposed the raw and brutal truth of war, shattering the myth of glorious battle and casting a pall over his ambition. It forced him to reconsider his vision of leadership and the cost he was willing to bear for his aspirations. It confronted him with the stark reality of his quest, nudging him to reflect upon the merits of a leader who led from the front, sharing the risks and bearing the losses.

As Pyrrhus stood on the brink of his hard-won victories, the ghosts of Heraclea and Asculum whispered the haunting echoes of a timeless wisdom – that the flames of ambition, left unchecked, can consume the very ones they seek to illuminate. His victories in Italy, paradoxical in their outcome, were a testament to the inherent contradictions of war, the capricious interplay of fate and free will, and the heavy toll of personal ambition.

To the onlookers, Pyrrhus was the victorious king, a beacon of Greek resistance against Roman aggression. Yet, to those who dared to look closer, he was also a poignant symbol of the paradox of warfare, a warrior who had tasted the bitter-sweet nectar of a Pyrrhic victory. His campaign in Italy, riddled with costly triumphs, not only transformed the strategic landscape of the Italian peninsula but also cast a profound impact on the very man who had dared to challenge the might of Rome.

In the final reckoning, Pyrrhus of Epirus emerged from the Italian campaign as a man forever changed by his victories. His perception of war, leadership, and personal ambition had undergone a profound transformation. He had begun his campaign as a stalwart of Greek ambition and ended as a symbol of the devastating cost of war, forever immortalized in the annals of history through the term that bore his name - Pyrrhic victory.

Even as Pyrrhus left the shores of Italy, he carried with him the haunting echoes of his victories, their memory indelibly etched into his soul. His reflection in the mirror of history revealed a figure who stood at the precipice of paradoxical triumphs, his name forever linked to the destructive dance of war and ambition. His journey served as a poignant reminder that the price of victory could sometimes overshadow its glory, casting a long shadow over the very ideals it sought to uphold. In the end, Pyrrhus of Epirus, the Warrior King, remained an enigmatic figure - a symbol of ambition, courage, and the high price of victory.

CHAPTER 13:

Gods and Omens: Religion and Myth in Pyrrhus' Life

From the earliest annals of human history, mankind has sought answers in the heavens and earth alike, entrusting their fate to a higher power, deeming the capriciousness of existence to be the whims of gods. Religion was a critical aspect of ancient societies, a divine compass that guided morality, politics, and personal lives. It painted the canvas of Greek life in vibrant hues of reverence, fear, awe, and wisdom, infusing their existence with a sense of purpose and destiny.

In the realm of Pyrrhus, the influence of the divine was palpable, steering the life of the Warrior King as much as his own free will. Gods were not merely ethereal beings living in some distant celestial realm; they were integral parts of everyday life, their presence felt in the rustling leaves, the raging storms, the mighty seas, and the valorous heart of a warrior. This chapter ventures into the spiritual realms of Pyrrhus, delving into his religious beliefs, the myths surrounding his life, and the omens that, in his eyes, signposted his destiny.

Pyrrhus, like his contemporaries, was a product of a society where the lines between religion and superstition were intriguingly blurred. From the womb to the tomb, life was an orchestrated symphony of religious rituals, prayers, and sacrifices, creating a cosmic rhythm that the Greeks danced to. The deities that ruled this world were as diverse as the phenomena they presided over. There were gods for war, wisdom, love, the sea, the underworld, and everything in between. And these gods, the Greeks believed, were deeply invested in the affairs of humans.

The pantheon of Pyrrhus' devotion was dominated by two figures – Zeus, the king of the gods, and Athena, the goddess of wisdom and war. It was said that Pyrrhus was a direct descendant of Achilles, the famed hero of the Trojan War, through his mother, Phthia. Achilles was the son of a sea-nymph Thetis, and thus the grandchild of Zeus. This divine lineage, woven into the fabric of Pyrrhus' identity, cast a divine aura on the King of Epirus, situating him within the broader narrative of the cosmic drama.

This lineage had a profound influence on Pyrrhus, inculcating a sense of divine destiny that shaped his worldview. He saw himself not as a mere mortal ruler but as an agent of Zeus, bound by a heavenly mandate to carry forward the heroic lineage of Achilles. He sought to mirror the bravery and martial prowess of his mythical ancestor, and this pursuit of valor influenced his decisions, whether he was strategizing a battle or ruling Epirus.

Similarly, Pyrrhus' admiration for Athena, the goddess of strategic warfare, reflected in his tactical acumen and his thirst for knowledge. Athena, often represented with an owl – the symbol of wisdom – was revered by Pyrrhus for her strategic skills and intellectual prowess. His coinage often bore the visage of Athena, a testament to the goddess's integral presence in his life and reign.

But the divine connection was not limited to reverent worship. It was a two-way street. The Greeks sought the guidance of the gods through oracles, divination, and omens, believing that these divine signals could reveal the future, guide decisions, or even change one's fate. Pyrrhus was no stranger to these practices. Anecdotes suggest that he relied on oracles and prophecies to navigate the tumultuous sea of his destiny.

One such prophecy had its roots in Pyrrhus' youth, during his days of uncertain exile. The Oracle of Delphi, the most prestigious in the Greek world, had foretold that Pyrrhus would eventually rise to power and that the 'Eagle' would one day claim his rightful place. This prophecy, seared into the young prince's mind, fuelled his ambitions, reassuring him in times of despair that his suffering was merely a prelude to greater glory.

The trust Pyrrhus placed in omens was equally striking. The presence of an eagle during important events of his life, such as his safe escape from an assassination attempt in Argos, was interpreted as a divine sign of Zeus' protection, reinforcing the prophecy of his rise. For Pyrrhus, these were not mere coincidences; they were divine scripts being played out, with him as the protagonist.

Yet, his faith in the divine was neither blind nor unidirectional. While he sought their favor, he also held them accountable. After his string of losses against Rome, Pyrrhus, in a fit of frustration, was said to have exclaimed, "O Hercules! How much easier it is to be a god than a general!" This exclamation revealed a fascinating aspect of Pyrrhus' relationship with the gods. They were his guides and patrons, but also the entities he questioned and challenged in times of anguish.

Such was the intertwining of faith and fate in Pyrrhus' life – a vivid illustration of the Greek world's sacred and secular interplay. From the heights of Olympus to the mortal realms of Epirus, the divine and human realms were interconnected, each influencing the other. Pyrrhus was a product of this interaction, his life a fascinating saga punctuated by the footprints of the gods.

Religion, for Pyrrhus, was a matter of faith and practicality, a divine validation of his lineage and destiny. The omens and prophecies were his cosmic roadmap, and the gods, his celestial companions in the journey. In the echoes of Zeus' thunder and Athena's wisdom, he found the reassurance and guidance that spurred him towards his extraordinary life.

But in the end, Pyrrhus was no pawn of divine whim. He strove to carve out his destiny with his decisions, his bravery, and his intellect, embodying the essence of human agency amidst divine determinism. Through the prism of Pyrrhus' life, we perceive a crucial lesson of history – the human and the divine, though appearing distinct, are intrinsically intertwined, each shaping the narrative of the other, in the grand tapestry of existence. The story of Pyrrhus is, thus, as much a tale of gods and omens as it is a chronicle of a warrior-king's life.

CHAPTER 14:

A Clash with Carthage: The Sicilian Campaign

From the land of Rome, where Pyrrhus had fought with grim determination, our narrative now carries us across the sea. The winds of destiny, like those of the Mediterranean, had their own whims and currents, carrying Pyrrhus towards a land of seductive charm and brutal reality—Sicily. Here, amidst its lemon groves and honeyed vineyards, unfolded the next chapter of Pyrrhus' life, a new arena where his mettle as a warrior and a king would be tested against a formidable adversary, Carthage.

From the heartlands of Africa, Carthage, an empire born of Phoenician grit, had stretched its arms towards the azure heart of the Mediterranean. At the time of Pyrrhus' arrival, the Punic state was already a formidable presence in the region, its dominion extending over much of the western Mediterranean, including the western part of Sicily.

Sicily, a triangular jewel set in the cerulean waters of the Mediterranean, was a land of contrasts. Its fertile plains and rolling hills made it a granary for the ancients, while the towering Mount Etna breathed a harsh reminder of nature's fickle temperament. The island was a melting pot of cultures—native Sicilians,

Greeks, Carthaginians, and others had left indelible prints on its sandy shores.

The year was 278 BCE when Pyrrhus set foot on Sicilian soil. His reputation as a formidable warrior had preceded him, carried on the wings of rumor and fear. The Sicilian Greeks, in the face of Carthaginian encroachments, had called out for his aid, hoping the Epirote King would be their savior. Pyrrhus, always the one to dance with destiny, had responded to the call. But the decision was not merely propelled by an altruistic desire to protect the Greek colonies; it bore the unmistakable stamp of strategic considerations.

Sicily presented a new theater of power for Pyrrhus, an opportunity to fortify his position in the Mediterranean and wrest a part of its control from Rome and Carthage. The island was also a stepping stone to Africa, a direct pathway to Carthage's heartlands. In the political chessboard of the time, securing Sicily was tantamount to gaining a queen—the game-changer.

Carthage, aware of the threat that Pyrrhus posed, was not a silent spectator. It was a matured empire, its strength forged in the crucible of commerce, naval power, and mercenary armies. Carthage's response was swift and unambiguous. This was a challenge they would not back away from. The stage was set for a new confrontation, one that would send ripples through the tranquil Mediterranean.

The campaign that ensued was a testament to the complexity of the times. Pyrrhus, fresh from the trials of Italy, was a seasoned commander. The harsh lessons from the battles against Rome had refined his strategies, and his respect for his enemy had grown. He knew that Carthage, with its naval prowess and extensive resources, was no pushover. Therefore, Pyrrhus knew his traditional strategies would not be enough—he had to adapt, to innovate, to improvise.

His tactics in Sicily displayed this remarkable flexibility. Realizing the crucial role of naval power in this new theatre of war, Pyrrhus augmented his fleet, leveraging the naval expertise of the Tarentines and other Greek allies. He realized that to conquer an island, he had to rule the seas. The Greek cities in Sicily, eager for liberation from the Carthaginian yoke, rallied under Pyrrhus' banner, providing him with the much-needed man power.

His campaign against Carthage was as much a psychological warfare as it was a military one. Pyrrhus knew that the Carthaginians, despite their vast resources, relied heavily on mercenaries. These were soldiers of fortune, who fought not for a homeland or an ideal, but for the promise of gold. Pyrrhus sought to use this to his advantage. His reputation as an invincible warrior, the stories of his bravery, and his charismatic leadership were deployed as weapons to demoralize and destabilize the Carthaginian ranks.

The battles that followed were a strange mix of conventional and unconventional warfare. At times, it was the sheer brute force of the phalanxes, the crushing charge of the war elephants, and the strategic genius of Pyrrhus that prevailed. At other times, it was stealth, subterfuge, and psychological warfare that tipped the scales.

The Battle of Heraclea Minoa, one of the key engagements of the campaign, encapsulated the dynamism of Pyrrhus' strategy. He ingeniously used his war elephants, a terrifying novelty for the Carthaginians, to break their lines, while his phalanxes, disciplined and deadly, made short work of the enemy. The Carthaginians were not only defeated; they were routed. The victory was a significant boost for Pyrrhus, reaffirming his invincibility in the eyes of his men and instilling a sense of dread in his enemies.

However, the path to victory was not a straight one. Pyrrhus faced resistance not only from Carthage but also from within. The Sicilian cities, initially welcoming his intervention, became increasingly wary of his ambitions. Their hopes for a liberator were beginning to fade, replaced by the dread of an emerging despot. Pyrrhus, the savior, was becoming Pyrrhus, the conqueror. The political dynamics of the island were shifting, the undercurrents of unrest bubbling beneath the surface.

Nevertheless, for the moment, Pyrrhus was in the ascendant. His strategic acumen, combined with the ferocity of his troops, were pushing the Carthaginians back. He was slowly but steadily gaining control over Sicily. But in the shadow of his victories, loomed a question—what was the price of this success? And was he ready to pay it?

The Sicilian campaign was not just a military expedition for Pyrrhus; it was a test of his adaptability, his ability to navigate through a complex web of cultural, political, and geographical challenges. It showed his willingness to evolve, to discard the familiar and embrace the unknown.

And yet, amidst the sweet taste of victories, there lingered a bitter aftertaste. The very people he had come to liberate were beginning to view him with suspicion, the weight of his ambitions casting a long, ominous shadow. Pyrrhus, always at home in the chaos of battle, was now caught in a different kind of chaos—one that threatened to undermine the foundations of his hard-earned victories.

As Pyrrhus gazed across the Mediterranean, the sun setting over the sea, he was aware that his battle for Sicily was far from over. The echo of war drums still hung in the air, the specter of Carthage still lurked in the horizon, and the grumblings of discontent still whispered in the wind. His trials were far from over; the enigma of Sicily was yet to be unraveled.

From the lands of Epirus to the mountains of Italy and now, to the shores of Sicily, Pyrrhus had journeyed far. But the true journey, he knew, was not one of distance but of understanding—understanding the complex dynamics of power, the intricate dance of diplomacy, and the unforgiving realities of leadership. And as the Sicilian campaign continued to unfold, Pyrrhus was becoming more than a warrior; he was growing into a strategist, a leader, a statesman.

CHAPTER 15:

Kingdom of the Sun: The Battle for Syracuse

There is a quality to Sicily that whispers ancient tales and breathes history into the wind that flutters through its landscapes. As the birthplace of Archimedes and the setting of the Odyssey's climactic scenes, the island has a storied past etched into its very soil. And within this island, a city emerged, resplendent and radiant, the proverbial crown jewel of Sicily—Syracuse. To control Syracuse was to grasp the heartbeat of Sicily, a prize much sought but seldom secured. Into this tapestry of power and history strode Pyrrhus, bringing with him the winds of change.

The year 276 BCE found Pyrrhus knee-deep in his Sicilian campaign. His battles against Carthage had seen successes, but Pyrrhus was not a man to rest on laurels. He saw in Syracuse not just a city but a symbol, the linchpin that could define his Sicilian endeavors. However, the Syracuse that Pyrrhus aimed to conquer was not merely a collection of stone and mortar. It was a living, breathing entity, as unpredictable and tempestuous as the sea that cradled it.

Syracuse was the beating heart of Hellenistic culture in Sicily, a testament to Greek ingenuity and resilience. But it was more than a city of aesthetics and philosophy—it was a fortress, guarded by natural and man-made fortifications. Ringed by the sea on one side and protected by sheer cliffs on the other, Syracuse was a challenging prize even for the most seasoned conqueror.

Pyrrhus, ever the tactician, was aware of this. He knew the intrinsic and strategic worth of Syracuse, but he also understood the daunting challenge that it represented. It was not just the walls of Syracuse he had to breach, but its spirit—the proud, unyielding spirit of a people fiercely protective of their freedom.

To secure Syracuse, Pyrrhus had to employ a mix of military prowess, diplomatic maneuvering, and psychological warfare. His reputation as a formidable warrior played a significant role, sowing seeds of fear among the enemy ranks. He further bolstered this image with displays of his military might, staging elaborate parades of his soldiers, his phalanxes, and, most significantly, his war elephants. These towering beasts, armored and terrible, were a spectacle designed to instill awe and terror in equal measure.

Yet, along with the specter of war, Pyrrhus offered the olive branch of peace. He understood the importance of winning hearts, not just battles. He reached out to the influential citizens of Syracuse, offering assurances of his respect for their laws and traditions, promising them autonomy and freedom from Carthaginian control. This was not merely a strategic move; it was a calculated gamble, a bid to win the city without resorting to a costly and destructive siege.

The strategy was sound, but the execution was fraught with difficulties. Syracuse was a city of many voices, and not all were willing to bow to the Epirote king. Resistance came in many forms—open defiance, subversive rumor-mongering, clandestine meetings—and Pyrrhus found himself fighting a shadowy enemy that was as elusive as it was persistent. This was not a battle fought in the open, beneath the gaze of the sun and the gods; it was a struggle that unfolded in the shadows of Syracuse, a test of Pyrrhus' patience and his understanding of human nature.

Amidst this, Pyrrhus did not neglect his military responsibilities. He strengthened his position around Syracuse, fortifying his camps and securing key strategic points. The Epirote king, despite his diplomatic efforts, was under no illusions—he knew that Syracuse might have to be taken by force.

And so, Pyrrhus found himself caught in a dance as old as time—a dance of war and diplomacy, power and persuasion. It was a delicate balance, a tightrope walk on the edge of a sword, and Pyrrhus, for all his martial prowess, was navigating uncharted waters.

Eventually, the Syracusean resistance waned. Perhaps it was the relentless pressure from Pyrrhus' troops, the seemingly invincible war elephants, or the subtle, patient diplomacy of the Epirote king. But, likely, it was a combination of all these factors. And so, Syracuse, the city of the sun, opened its gates to Pyrrhus, the warrior king from Epirus.

But the victory was as bitter as it was sweet. Pyrrhus might have won Syracuse, but at what cost? The city he now ruled was not the vibrant, unbroken jewel he had coveted; it was a city divided, its spirit bruised by the fear of war and the reality of foreign rule. And as the sun set over Syracuse, casting long, solemn shadows, Pyrrhus knew that the real challenge had just begun. He had won Syracuse, but could he win the hearts of its people?

The battle for Syracuse was not just a military campaign; it was a critical turning point in Pyrrhus' Sicilian expedition. It was an indication of the evolving landscape of the island, the shifting dynamics of power, and a measure of Pyrrhus' adaptability. It was a victory, yes, but it was also a warning—a reminder that the path to power was littered with unforeseen challenges.

As the echoes of battle faded and the dust settled, Syracuse bore the indelible imprint of Pyrrhus—the mark of a conqueror, a liberator, and a king. Yet, this was a chapter in the city's story, not its conclusion. For Pyrrhus, the real task had just begun—transforming Syracuse from a conquered city into an integral part of his Sicilian realm.

In the grand narrative of Pyrrhus' life, Syracuse stands as a milestone—a testament to his military genius, his diplomatic acumen, and his relentless pursuit of power. Yet, it also serves as a stark reminder of the cost of ambition—the price that must be paid in blood, sweat, and trust. As the Kingdom of the Sun, Syracuse was not just a city; it was a symbol—a beacon of hope for some, a specter of fear for others. And as Pyrrhus would soon discover, symbols, much like cities, are not easily controlled.

CHAPTER 16:

The Tides of Fortune: The Return to Italy

In the annals of history, there is an ebb and flow—a ceaseless tide—that marks the fortunes of men. A king may ride the crest of victory one moment, only to be pulled under by the currents of defeat the next. The life of Pyrrhus, the Epirote king, embodied this undulating rhythm of history with a stark clarity.

Pyrrhus had tasted both the sweet nectar of victory and the bitter gall of defeat in his Sicilian campaign. Syracuse, the crown jewel of the island, had been won, but the conquest had left the city's spirit bruised and its people divided. Yet, Pyrrhus, ever the ambitious king, was not one to dwell on past glories or missteps. His gaze was firmly set on the horizon, on the next strategic gambit. And so, as the sun set on Syracuse, Pyrrhus cast his lot with the tides of fortune, setting his sights back on Italy.

The decision to return to Italy was not impulsive but rather a calculated strategic move. Pyrrhus had left the mainland under the strain of his costly victories against the Romans, famously giving rise to the term 'Pyrrhic victory.' But the Epirote king was no stranger to adversity. He was, after all, a seasoned warrior, a tactician molded in the crucible of combat and honed by the harsh lessons of war. He was also a pragmatist, keenly aware that the shifting political and military landscape of Italy provided fresh opportunities.

But what were the considerations that led Pyrrhus back to the Italian peninsula? What were the allure and the challenge of Italy that drew him back into the fray? A closer look at the factors at play offers a window into the mind of the king.

Pyrrhus was not blind to the growing might of Rome. He had clashed with the Republic's legions before and had seen firsthand their resilience and military prowess. Yet, he was also cognizant of the fact that Rome, while formidable, was not invincible. The Republic was in its ascendancy, a young power with ambitions that outpaced its grasp. It was embroiled in wars on multiple fronts, struggling to exert control over the fractious Italian tribes. This state of flux was a weakness that Pyrrhus, ever the opportunist, sought to exploit.

Moreover, the Greek colonies in southern Italy, from where Pyrrhus had initially been invited to intervene, still looked upon the Epirote king as a potential liberator. Their hopes had not dimmed, their need for an ally against Rome not lessened. These Greek city-states offered Pyrrhus a base from which he could launch his renewed Italian campaign.

Finally, there was the matter of Tarentum. The city-state had been the original catalyst for Pyrrhus' Italian intervention. He had left Tarentum in the hands of his trusted generals when he had ventured to Sicily. However, the news that reached Pyrrhus in Syracuse spoke of unrest and uncertainty in Tarentum. It seemed that the city's rulers were chafing under Epirote control, their loyalties wavering. Pyrrhus understood the strategic importance of Tarentum—the port city was a gateway to Italy, a vital link in his Adriatic ambitions. The potential loss of Tarentum was a risk Pyrrhus could ill afford.

Thus, the return to Italy was not a reckless charge into the unknown. It was a calculated risk, a strategic pivot to leverage Rome's distractions, the goodwill of the Greek colonies, and the vital importance of Tarentum.

Yet, the path before Pyrrhus was not an easy one. The Romans had not been idle during his Sicilian sojourn. They had fortified their positions, built alliances, and honed their military might. The Italy that Pyrrhus was returning to was not the one he had left. The Romans were no longer the untested foe he had faced in his earlier campaigns. They had learned from their clashes with Pyrrhus, adapted their tactics, and emerged a more formidable adversary.

Moreover, the Greek city-states of southern Italy, while still supportive of Pyrrhus, were wary. The Epirote king's departure for Sicily had left them in the lurch, facing the Roman threat without their champion. There were lingering doubts, questions about Pyrrhus' commitment to their cause. He would need to assuage these concerns, reaffirm his alliances, and reestablish his credentials as a defender of Greek interests in Italy.

And then, there was Tarentum. The city-state was a tinderbox of political tension, its leaders grappling with divided loyalties and the weight of Epirote rule. Pyrrhus would need to navigate this complex political landscape, temper the brewing unrest, and reassert his control over the city.

These were the challenges that awaited Pyrrhus as he turned his gaze back towards Italy. They were formidable, certainly, but not insurmountable. Pyrrhus was, after all, a seasoned warrior and a pragmatic strategist. He understood the dynamics of power, the nuances of alliances, and the rhythms of war. He knew how to wield the carrot and the stick, to inspire and intimidate in equal measure.

The return to Italy marked a new phase in Pyrrhus' Italian campaign, a renewed push in the grand chess game of power. It was a testament to the Epirote king's ambition, his resilience, and his knack for seizing opportunities amidst the flux of fortunes.

Yet, it was also a reminder of the capricious tides of history. Pyrrhus, the warrior king, was once again riding the crest of ambition, steering his course through the currents of conflict. Yet, the sea of history is a fickle mistress. The tides of fortune can turn swiftly, and the waves of adversity can rise abruptly. As Pyrrhus plotted his course back to Italy, he was stepping into the cauldron of history, a theatre of conflict where victory and defeat are but two sides of the same coin.

It was a challenge that Pyrrhus embraced with his characteristic determination. He was a warrior king, a veteran of many battles. He knew that the road to power was not a straight path, but a twisting labyrinth fraught with peril and opportunity. His return to Italy was a testament to his indomitable spirit, his unyielding resolve, and his ceaseless quest for glory.

The sun set on Syracuse as Pyrrhus set his sights on Italy, the waters of the Adriatic a shimmering pathway to a new campaign. And as the Epirote king turned his gaze towards the horizon, the tides of fortune ebbed and flowed, the ceaseless rhythm of history playing out in the grand theatre of the ancient world. It was the dawn of a new chapter in the epic saga of Pyrrhus, the warrior king—a chapter that would test his mettle, challenge his prowess, and etch his name into the annals of history.

CHAPTER 17:

Benevolent Despot or Tyrant? Assessing Pyrrhus' Rule

Every tale of heroism, every saga of an indomitable warrior, begs the question: what are the virtues that define a leader, a king? The bold strokes of a general, the delicate stratagems of a politician, and the enigmatic dance of diplomacy - these are the threads that weave the fabric of leadership. Yet, as we delve into the life of Pyrrhus, we tread on less certain ground, a shadowy intersection where the light of benevolence diffuses into the dark hues of tyranny.

Pyrrhus - a king, a conqueror, a philosopher. The pulse of his rule still reverberates through time, echoing the patterns of a melody both mellifluous and discordant. To listen to it is to sift through the coarse grains of historical narrative and conjecture, seeking the slender threads of truth. It's a symphony conducted in minor, in the somber key of power, a power both liberating and enslaving, harnessed by a man of profound complexity.

The king of Epirus was not merely a figure cast in bronze, frozen in the epic pose of battle, spear aloft, eyes aflame with ambition. His heart bore the weight of his people, a weight not lightened by conquest or glory, but deepened with the groaning plight of those he governed.

The hammer of history tends to flatten such figures, reducing them to two dimensions - the savior or the oppressor, the tyrant or the liberator. Pyrrhus resists this simplistic mould. He exists as a paradox, a benevolent despot whose rule is as intricate and nuanced as the man himself.

The measure of a ruler lies not solely in the wake of his battles, but in the way he governs in times of peace. The echo of swords clashing, the thunder of hooves, and the roar of victory - these are but mere fragments of the tapestry of leadership. And, in these quieter threads, in the silence between the stanzas of war, we discover another facet of Pyrrhus.

In the rugged lands of Epirus, against the backdrop of verdant hills and silver-flecked seas, Pyrrhus carved a kingdom that aspired toward the ideal of a philosopher's state. His hand, once clasping the sword hilt, now held the stylus of administration, his grip no less firm. Law and governance were his new weapons, his strategy not of conquest, but of growth and prosperity.

He invested in the infrastructure, overseeing the construction of roads that crisscrossed his kingdom, the arteries that brought life to Epirus. Commerce flourished under his reign, nurtured by his policies of free trade. He promoted the arts, and philosophers and poets found a patron in the king, a man whose appreciation for intellectual pursuits was as deep as his passion for war.

Education was not a privilege confined to the elite, but a right extended to the citizens of Epirus. Pyrrhus encouraged learning, fostering a spirit of intellectual curiosity. The youth of Epirus, boys and girls alike, were instructed in the arts and sciences, instilling in them not only the knowledge of their ancestors but the wisdom to question, to seek, to explore. It was a kingdom flourishing under the light of Hellenistic knowledge, nourished by the rivers of enlightenment and growth.

Yet, this benevolent visage of Pyrrhus should not overshadow the darker shades of his rule. His ambition, the thirst that propelled his armies across the Adriatic, was not quenched by the placid waters of peacetime. Pyrrhus was a conqueror, a master of the battlefield, and the taste of victory was a potent brew.

For all his investment in the people of Epirus, Pyrrhus was no stranger to the chilling grip of autocracy. The choices of his reign, the direction of his policies, rested solely in his hands. His word was law, unchallenged and unyielding. His decisions, even when seemingly benign, bore the mark of a single mind, a single will. His was a rule not of consensus but of command, a leadership style that strayed dangerously close to tyranny.

The people of Epirus, even as they reaped the rewards of Pyrrhus' policies, lived under the constant shadow of his authority. Dissent was not a choice, but a risk, a dare against a king whose wrath was as formidable as his generosity. For some, Pyrrhus was a beacon of progress, a king who brought prosperity to their lands. For others, he was an iron fist, an autocrat whose reign was a testament to unchecked power.

In the twilight dance of historical analysis, Pyrrhus casts a complex shadow. He was a king of contrasts, a figure of profound duality. He was a general whose strategies echoed on the battlefield, a leader whose influence rippled through the quiet currents of peacetime. Yet, he was also a despot, a ruler whose decisions bore the cold mark of tyranny.

In his grand theatre of rule, Pyrrhus played both parts with compelling conviction: the benevolent leader and the stern autocrat. His reign was a performance, a spectacle that spanned the spectrum from light to shadow, a chiaroscuro of power and ambition.

The question we're left grappling with, in the dust of his rule, is whether Pyrrhus was a benevolent king or a despotic tyrant. But perhaps that is the wrong question. Pyrrhus was not one or the other. He was both. And in that tension, in that dance between light and shadow, we find the true measure of Pyrrhus of Epirus.

To parse the character of such a man, to distill his essence into the clear liquor of historical truth, is a task fraught with challenge. Pyrrhus, in his ambition, in his generosity, in his tyranny, eludes the simplistic categories of benevolent or despot. His rule, like his life, was a complex mosaic, a tapestry of power woven from threads of diverse hues. It is this tapestry, intricate and sprawling, that is the true testament to his reign. It is not a tale of absolutes, but of shades and nuances, of a king who was both a beacon of progress and a symbol of autocracy.

Thus, Pyrrhus of Epirus remains a riddle wrapped in the enigma of his rule, a mystery we continue to unravel as we journey through the fog-shrouded realm of history. He was a benevolent despot, a figure of contradiction, a testament to the dual nature of power. He was Pyrrhus, the king, the warrior, the philosopher - the man whose rule etched a complex pattern in the sands of time, a pattern as intricate and enduring as the man himself.

CHAPTER 18:

Warrior King: Pyrrhus at War

As the smoke of the recent Italian campaign still lingered on his bronze armour, Pyrrhus stood, a figure worthy of the Homeric heroes of old. The magnanimity of his soul, matched only by his strategic acumen and fiery bravery, Pyrrhus, the king of Epirus, was also its fiercest warrior.

The brilliance of Pyrrhus in war was as multifaceted as the Mediterranean Sea itself. Let us dissect this prismatic mastery, this layered essence of warfare that Pyrrhus encapsulated, beginning with a critical understanding of his military philosophy.

A warrior at heart, Pyrrhus inherited the mantle of war early on. The battles fought, the exile survived, the alliances built, and the thrones reclaimed, all culminated into a mosaic of military experiences that lent him an understanding of war that was as broad as it was deep. His was not a mere rehashing of war tales heard from seasoned veterans or tactical norms gleaned from the pages of strategic treatises. Rather, it was a philosophy that lived and breathed, that evolved with each victory claimed and every defeat endured.

In the heart of his military doctrine lay a principle of audacity and action. A disdain for stagnancy was ingrained in Pyrrhus' approach to war, often to the point of recklessness, some critics would argue. Yet, this boldness was not an unguided arrow shot in the dark; it was a calculated risk born of confidence and military expertise.

His military strategy, honed in the crucible of countless conflicts, favoured not a blind offensive but a judicious mix of attack and defence. Recognising that every battlefield presented a unique array of opportunities and obstacles, Pyrrhus was known for his fluid battle plans, which, like water, could adapt and flow around the contours of the situation at hand. His was a strategy of flexibility, of anticipation, and of seizing the moment when it arrived.

His penchant for using combined arms, leveraging the strengths of infantry, cavalry, and elephants alike, echoed his understanding of the importance of versatility in warfare. Each arm had its function, its role in the greater scheme of the war machine, and Pyrrhus, the astute tactician, knew well how to orchestrate this symphony of violence and valor.

Yet, what distinguished Pyrrhus as a warrior king was not merely his military intellect or tactical genius. The spark that ignited his warfare philosophy was his unwavering bravery. He was no king that watched battles from afar, perched on a high vantage point, safely distanced from the blood and grime of the battlefield. No, Pyrrhus was a warrior king, his place was amongst his men, his hands stained with the same blood and dust that coated the soldiers' blades.

Remembered for his personal bravery, Pyrrhus was often found in the thick of the battle, wielding his lance with deadly precision and strength, a lion amongst wolves. His presence on the battlefield did not merely function as an inspiring beacon for his troops, but it also instilled a sense of shared destiny between the king and his soldiers, reinforcing the collective nature of their war efforts.

Such was the tenacity of his courage that, in the heat of battle, he often seemed oblivious to personal danger, risking his life with a seeming nonchalance that veiled a deep-seated commitment to his cause. While some saw this as foolhardy, others revered him as the embodiment of valour, the perfect warrior king leading by example.

Yet, the warrior in Pyrrhus was not without his weaknesses, not immune to the inherent follies that plague men of power. The same audacity that saw him through numerous victories also paved the way for crushing defeats. Pyrrhus, for all his battlefield prowess, was often seen as a risk-taker, a gambler who staked everything on the throw of the war-dice.

His impulsive nature, that leap-before-you-look tendency, often pushed him into ventures without fully understanding the long-term consequences. His campaigns in Italy and Sicily, undertaken without a thorough analysis of the strategic and logistical challenges, serve as prime examples of this.

On the other side of the spectrum, Pyrrhus, the man who dared to challenge Rome, was an innovator. The notable use of elephants in his battles brought a new dimension to Hellenistic warfare. These walking war towers, with their massive stature and destructive power, lent a psychological edge to his armies, and were a testament to Pyrrhus' adaptability and openness to embrace unconventional tactics.

Yet, the man who strode across battlefields with an air of invincibility was, at his core, human. Prone to overconfidence, his optimism often miscalculated the strength of his enemies, leading him to underestimate the sheer tenacity of Rome during his Italian campaigns. In his quest for glory, Pyrrhus also showed a lack of strategic patience, an eagerness to grasp victory, and an inability to see the forest for the trees.

Ultimately, the image of Pyrrhus, the warrior king, is a tableau of contrasts. It is the image of a man who was as audacious in his military strategies as he was brave on the battlefield. It is the image of a king who led from the front, who fought with his men, and who bore the same scars that they did. Yet, it is also an image of a man who, despite his brilliance, was flawed, whose overconfidence led to critical misjudgments, and whose audacious nature often outpaced his strategic considerations.

In the grand tapestry of history, Pyrrhus stands as a paragon of the warrior king, an emblem of bravery, strategic acumen, and personal engagement in warfare. Yet, in his strengths and his weaknesses, he is a poignant reminder of the human condition, that even in the realms of greatness, there exists a canvas of contradictions, a dialectic of heroism and folly. In the end, Pyrrhus was not merely a great king or a skilled warrior, he was a symbol of the enduring human spirit in the face of war, a testament to the age-old dance of strategy and strength, courage and calamity, victory and defeat.

CHAPTER 19:

Pyrrhus and the Hellenistic World

We know Pyrrhus to be a king, a philosopher, a fearsome warrior, but Pyrrhus was also a dancer – a dancer on the grand stage of the Hellenistic world. For there was a dance of sorts in the 3rd century BCE, a volatile pas de deux among rising and waning powers, interspersed with thrilling pirouettes of politics and deadly duels of warfare. Pyrrhus, the king of Epirus, was one of its most fascinating performers, whose steps, often out of rhythm with the conventional choreography, left an indelible mark on the Hellenistic ballet.

The canvas of the Hellenistic world was, to use Plutarch's metaphor, 'a vast theatre.' In this dramatic realm, Pyrrhus emerged not just as an actor, but a playwright of sorts, shaping and being shaped by the script of the age.

By the time Pyrrhus ascended to the throne of Epirus, the Hellenistic world was a symphony of city-states, kingdoms, and empires, all tuned to the rhythm of Alexander's legacy. The kingdoms of Macedonia, Egypt, and Seleucid Asia, born from the splinters of Alexander's empire, were all vying for dominance in this intricate geopolitical dance.

The choreography was no less complex on the smaller stage of Greece, a volatile mix of city-states and leagues, including Pyrrhus' own homeland of Epirus. It was a world defined by alliances as fragile as porcelain, wars that scorched the earth, and the constant churn of power dynamics.

From the outset, Pyrrhus saw the delicate balance of power in the Hellenistic world as both a challenge and an opportunity. He saw the endless possibilities for alliances and rivalries, the fluid borders ripe for expansion, and the volatile politics that offered a chance for a skilled statesman to rise. And rise Pyrrhus did.

Among his most significant alliances was that with Ptolemy I of Egypt. Pyrrhus arrived in Egypt as a young exile but soon gained the favor of the powerful Ptolemaic court. This relationship would prove instrumental in Pyrrhus' ascendancy to power, particularly the assistance he received in his successful bid to reclaim the Epirote throne.

Yet, the dance of Hellenistic alliances demanded a delicate balance of footwork, with each step carrying the risk of upsetting the volatile equilibrium. Pyrrhus would learn this lesson all too well. As Plutarch puts it, he was "like a player who cannot keep his hold, but is always spinning the ball to others." Such was the game of alliances in the Hellenistic world, and such were the perils Pyrrhus had to navigate.

His alliance with the Aetolian League, for instance, illustrates the intricate dance of diplomacy in the Hellenistic age. A powerful confederation of Greek city-states, the Aetolian League was a formidable player on the Hellenistic stage. Pyrrhus, recognizing their strategic value, sought to form an alliance. But such a partnership would not come without costs, as it strained his relations with Macedonia and ultimately triggered a fresh cycle of war.

Pyrrhus also formed alliances with city-states in Southern Italy and Sicily. Most notable was his alliance with Tarentum against Rome. The Tarentines, fearful of the growing Roman power, invited Pyrrhus to lead them, setting the stage for his legendary Italian campaigns.

Pyrrhus' diplomatic footwork was not limited to forming alliances. It also involved enmity, and on this dance floor, Pyrrhus had no shortage of adversaries. His most formidable was perhaps Rome, a rising power that Pyrrhus would famously challenge in his Italian campaign. Rome was Pyrrhus' nemesis, his equal in a dance of war that would see some of the most brutal and costly battles of the era.

The Hellenistic world was also a stage for cultural and intellectual exchange, and here too, Pyrrhus left his mark. From the teachings of Epicurus that shaped his philosophy to the military tactics learned from the Macedonians, Pyrrhus absorbed a plethora of influences from the wider Hellenistic world. These shaped not only his personal development but also his rule over Epirus, where he sought to synthesize these disparate elements into a coherent whole.

In this dance of the Hellenistic world, Pyrrhus was not merely a participant; he was an influencer. His military successes, particularly against Rome, reverberated across the Hellenistic world and earned him a reputation as a formidable leader. His tactics, particularly his effective use of elephants in battle, influenced the military strategies of his contemporaries.

His philosophy of kingship, too, rippled across the Hellenistic world. His belief in ruling with the consent of the governed, his concept of the 'philosopher king,' his diplomatic savvy - these all painted a vivid picture of Hellenistic rulership, influencing his contemporaries and successors alike.

Yet, Pyrrhus' dance in the Hellenistic world was not without missteps. His relentless pursuit of glory, his constant search for new conquests, often led him into wars that drained his resources and strained his alliances. His unwillingness to consolidate his gains, his inability to sustain lasting peace - these would ultimately cost him his life and his kingdom.

Pyrrhus' dance in the Hellenistic world was a complex ballet, a performance that captivated audiences far and wide. But like all performances, it came to an end. Yet, in this grand dance of history,

Pyrrhus' steps continue to echo, shaping our understanding of this fascinating era and the man who was its most compelling performer.

CHAPTER 20:

The Return to Epirus and the War with Macedonia

There is a compelling rhythm to the life of Pyrrhus - a primal beat that evokes the thunderous hooves of horses charging into battle, the triumphal fanfare of victory, the low hum of intrigue, and the melancholy echoes of loss. The contours of his life were moulded not just by the triumphs he enjoyed, but also by the poignant returns to his homeland. Each homecoming was punctuated with an almost Homeric tone, the narrative woven with shades of myth, glory, ambition, and a burning quest to leave an indelible mark on the annals of time.

By the time Pyrrhus returned to Epirus, the swirling sands of the hourglass had yielded a man whose destiny was as intricately intertwined with his kingdom as the vines of the wine-loving god Dionysus were with the fertile Epirote land. The face of Pyrrhus reflected both the marble-like resolve of a leader and the finely chiselled complexities of a man navigating the intricate web of Hellenistic politics. As he stepped once again onto the land of his ancestors, he was no longer a young exile returning from the court of Glaukias, nor was he the ambitious king who had set out for the conquests in Italy and Sicily. He was a seasoned leader, a tested warrior, and a man hardened by the relentless grind of ambition and warfare.

His return to Epirus was not a retreat, but a tactical manoeuvre, a pivot from the western Mediterranean to the volatile theatres of the East. He came back bearing the wealth of Italy and Sicily, the hard-won spoils of war, and an enhanced reputation as a military leader. But the Mediterranean world Pyrrhus returned to was drastically different from the one he had left behind. The region was no longer simply a stage for his dreams of grandeur; it was a living, breathing theatre where ambitions, alliances, and animosities created a dynamic - often volatile - geopolitical tableau.

The thunderous drumbeat of Pyrrhus's destiny led him straight into a confrontation with Antigonus II Gonatas, the stoic king of Macedonia. The region's history was deeply intertwined with Epirus, its legacy intricately connected to Pyrrhus's lineage. To understand this engagement's magnitude, one must delve into the labyrinthine dynamics that shaped the relationship between Epirus, Macedonia, and their respective kings.

Antigonus II, the one-time ally and now a formidable opponent, was a man who wore his Macedonian pride like a finely wrought suit of armour. The Gonatas suffix to his name was a proud nod to his father, Demetrius Poliorcetes, the 'Besieger' - a lineage that endowed him with an intimate understanding of the theatrics of power. The Macedonia that Antigonus ruled was a realm that had been under the towering shadow of Alexander the Great, bearing the dual burden of its glorious past and uncertain future.

Pyrrhus, the Molossian shepherd turned philosopher-king, now locked horns with Antigonus, the Macedonian royal whose realm was bequeathed to him through a lineage of conquerors. It was a clash that was not only about territories or power but also a contest of differing visions for the Hellenistic world.

Their first confrontation occurred at the Battle of Aous in 274 BC. Aous, the river which, according to lore, was named after the mythical charioteer of the solar deity Helios, bore silent testimony to the clash of these two titans. Pyrrhus, drawing on his military experience and armed with his infamous war elephants, managed to push back Antigonus' forces, forcing them into a tactical retreat. It was a victory for Pyrrhus, but one that was not without its price. The battle saw the dwindling of his veteran troops and the inevitable thinning of his once formidable force of war elephants.

The Pyrrhic victories of the past were catching up to him. Although he held the battlefield, he was left with a significantly depleted force. Nevertheless, Pyrrhus, the eternally optimistic warrior, saw it as an opportunity to advance into Macedonia. Antigonus, the crafty statesman, utilised his political acumen and understanding of Macedonia's terrain to wage a war of attrition that tested Pyrrhus's dwindling resources.

In the years that followed, Pyrrhus found himself grappling with the demands of a large kingdom, the logistical complexities of warfare, and the constant need to maintain his alliances. He was far from the youthful king who had once dreamt of emulating the likes of Alexander the Great. He was now a seasoned leader, a warrior who had weathered the trials of numerous battles, a king who had tasted the bitter tang of losses and the intoxicating sweetness of victories.

Despite his aspirations and the initial successes, the shadow of the Macedonian war loomed over his reign like an insurmountable mountain peak. The Epirote king was slowly learning the challenging lesson of the ebb and flow of fortune. His vision of a united Hellenistic realm was fraying at the edges, the bright tapestry of his dreams gradually losing colour under the harsh sun of reality. And yet, amid the difficulties, the flame of ambition still flickered in the heart of Pyrrhus, its light reflecting in the determined set of his jaw and the resolute gleam of his eyes.

The war with Macedonia was a significant chapter in the tumultuous narrative of Pyrrhus's life. It marked the beginning of a protracted conflict that would test his military prowess and his capacity as a ruler. His return to Epirus, the land that cradled him in his youth, saw him navigate a tumultuous period fraught with battles, tactical manoeuvres, political machinations, and shifting alliances. The amphitheatre of the Hellenistic world was a grand stage where the acts of history were being played out, and Pyrrhus, ever the protagonist, had a role that was far from over.

This period of his life, marked by the war with Macedonia, stands as a testament to the capricious nature of fortune and the relentless march of time. The man who stood on the threshold of his kingdom, gazing out at the land he loved, was a king who had tasted the intoxicating wine of victory and the bitter gall of defeat. His experiences had moulded him into a figure whose legacy would echo down the corridors of time, whispering tales of a king, a warrior, and a philosopher whose life was as fascinating as it was tumultuous. His story, like the river Aous, flowed ceaselessly onward, twisting and turning through the landscape of history, its current bearing the indelible mark of the legendary King Pyrrhus of Epirus.

CHAPTER 21:

Strained Alliances: Pyrrhus and the Aetolian League

There's something exquisitely heartbreaking in observing a strong friendship crumble. Bonds that once braced individuals in their most vulnerable moments, when frayed, leave behind a haunting echo of lost kinship. This is the story of Pyrrhus of Epirus and the Aetolian League, a tale of the fraying of alliances, enmeshed in the intricate network of Hellenistic geopolitics.

The Aetolian League, a confederation of tribes and city-states nestled in the rugged mountains of central Greece, emerged as a formidable force in the wake of Alexander's death. Their lands, stretching from the Ionian Sea to the Gulf of Corinth, were a lattice of fortified cities and sacred sanctuaries. Eager to take their place in the post-Alexandrian world, they found an ally in Pyrrhus.

Pyrrhus, for his part, needed friends. His kingdom of Epirus, while grand in its natural beauty, was a geopolitical minnow amidst the whale-like empires of the Hellenistic age. Thus, he courted the Aetolians, this coalition of tribes and city-states that commanded the attention of Macedonia and even distant Rome.

It was an alliance of pragmatism, born out of the realities of the fractured world they inhabited. As Plutarch noted, "Pyrrhus, a wise king, knew to respect the potential of small allies." Their initial dealings were courteous, and there was a feeling of mutual benefit. The Epirotes and the Aetolians held joint military exercises, exchanged diplomatic envoys, and pledged to stand together in the face of aggression.

Yet, as the saying goes, power is a curious beast. Pyrrhus' victories in Italy, while costly, had inflated his image. He was no longer just the king of Epirus. He was Pyrrhus, the slayer of Romans, the conqueror of Sicily, the new Alexander. In his rise, the delicate balance of his alliance with the Aetolians started to wobble.

The Aetolians, a hardy folk with a proud warrior tradition, were known for their independence. They did not take kindly to the notion of becoming subservient to Pyrrhus. Their resentment grew with every tale of his exploits that crossed the Ionian Sea. The alliance began to show the first signs of strain.

In 275 BC, an event occurred that tore the fabric of this alliance. A trivial disagreement over spoils of war spiraled into a diplomatic incident. The incident was an affront to Pyrrhus' pride, who viewed it as a challenge to his authority. Tempers flared, insults were hurled, and a bond that had once seemed unbreakable started to unravel.

Pyrrhus, the eternal warrior, reacted as he knew best. He gathered his forces and prepared for a punitive campaign against the Aetolian League. The stage was set for a confrontation that would further roil the already turbulent waters of the Hellenistic world.

Meanwhile, the Aetolians, not ones to be browbeaten, prepared their defenses. Their hill forts bristled with spears and their war cries echoed through the valleys. A standoff ensued, with Pyrrhus' army on one side of the Pindus mountains and the Aetolians on the other.

Yet, war never came. Pyrrhus, ever the pragmatist, realized the folly of fighting a war on two fronts. He had the threat of Rome looming in the west and a potential war with his former ally in the east. The specter of a Pyrrhic victory hung over his decision.

Thus, Pyrrhus chose diplomacy over the battlefield. A series of negotiations followed, with Pyrrhus demonstrating a side of him seldom seen – the patient negotiator. The two sides reached a tenuous agreement, restoring a semblance of their previous alliance.

The strains, however, remained. The Aetolians would always view Pyrrhus with a mix of admiration and resentment. Pyrrhus, on the other hand, learned a harsh lesson about the fickleness of alliances. His relationship with the Aetolian League became a mirror reflecting the complex dynamics of the Hellenistic world, where friends could become foes at the drop of a helmet.

As we contemplate the intricacies of Pyrrhus' alliance with the Aetolian League, one cannot help but feel a pang of sadness. Here were two powers, brought together by circumstance and mutual benefit, driven apart by pride and ambition. This alliance, once the cornerstone of Pyrrhus' Hellenistic diplomacy, became a symbol of the volatile nature of alliances in the fractured world following Alexander's death.

We are left with the image of Pyrrhus, standing on the precipice of a decision, gazing upon the rugged landscapes of Aetolia. Here was a warrior, a king, a philosopher, struggling to navigate the labyrinth of alliances and enmities that defined his world.

The tale of Pyrrhus and the Aetolian League is ultimately a reflection of the world they inhabited. It was a world of flux, where the sands of power constantly shifted underfoot, and where alliances were as brittle as they were crucial. In the grand stage of the Hellenistic world, the story of Pyrrhus and the Aetolian League remains a poignant reminder of the perils of ambition, the fragility of alliances, and the indomitable spirit of independence.

CHAPTER 22:

The Twilight Years: Pyrrhus' Later Reign

In a world where power was won by the strength of a warrior's sword and the strategic acuity of a king's mind, Pyrrhus of Epirus navigated through his twilight years with a potent cocktail of force and guile. These were times that tested the mettle of the warrior king, times that highlighted his extraordinary capacity to adapt to an ever-shifting landscape, and yet, times that illuminated the delicate fragility of his rule.

The Epirus of this epoch was like an amphitheater, reverberating with the echoes of past glories and casting long, ominous shadows of potential threats. Pyrrhus, the principal player in this grand performance, was a man, who, like a mighty river, shaped his own course even as he was moulded by the terrains of destiny.

At the helm, Pyrrhus was now a seasoned player in the world stage, a lion in winter, whose golden mane still bore streaks of fierce radiance. His profile was chisselled by years of battle and strategy, victories and setbacks. And like a well-aged wine, his rule had ripened, exhibiting the nuanced complexity of an extraordinary life spent in pursuit of glory and power.

Our story unfurls in the latter half of his reign, when the sage-like hues of diplomacy began to play more prominently in Pyrrhus' palette of rulership. His court was alive with intrigue, pulsating with the energies of various factions, each seeking to influence the king, who sat at the nexus of their ambitions. He was a lighthouse in the tumultuous seas of Epirus politics, the singular point of focus for every ship, no matter how storm-tossed or directionless.

The murmuring tongues of envoys, emissaries, spies and conspirators created an ever-evolving symphony, a rhapsody of power that played out in the court's opulent chambers. Their whispers were like hidden currents in the ocean, unseen yet potent, capable of turning the tide or capsizing the unprepared. Pyrrhus, however, was a master navigator, steering his ship of state with deftness borne from a lifetime of leadership.

And yet, the world outside his court was not static. The larger Hellenistic world was akin to a multi-headed Hydra, a complex, multi-faceted creature, its different heads symbolising the diverse and often conflicting states that comprised it. This was a realm that demanded a ruler who could wrestle with the Hydra without being devoured by it. Pyrrhus, true to his Homeric hero-like stature, embraced this challenge with unwavering resilience.

The external relations of Pyrrhus' kingdom were a series of carefully strung pearls, each a treaty or an alliance that glistened with promises of support or threats of hostility. The bonds with the Aetolian League and the delicate dance with Macedonia marked his regional diplomacy, while the simmering tension with Rome added a dash of unseasoned spice to this elaborate dish.

During these years, Pyrrhus became more than just a warrior; he embodied the role of a diplomat, strategist, and visionary. But amidst the grandeur and glory, a more intimate portrait of Pyrrhus also emerged. Here was a ruler who cherished the camaraderie of his comrades, a king who found solace in the company of his loyal Molossian hound, a father who watched over his sons with hawk-like protectiveness.

His sons, born of his marriages, were now maturing into their own personas, echoing different aspects of their father's complex character. Alexandros, his eldest, was a chip off the old block, showing a fierce passion for military prowess and statecraft. His younger sons, Ptolemy and Helenus, exhibited a keen interest in the diplomatic aspects of rulership, reflecting the evolving dimensions of Pyrrhus' own reign.

Yet, this familial portrait was not untouched by strains of discord. As much as Pyrrhus was a king and a warrior, he was also a man susceptible to the vulnerabilities of human emotions. In his later years, the tides of suspicion and doubt started to wash over the shores of his trust, particularly regarding the ambitions of his sons. Alexandros' growing popularity started casting long shadows on Pyrrhus' psyche, generating ripples of unease that subtly yet irrevocably began to influence the court's dynamics.

Pyrrhus' reign was a vibrant tapestry, a weave of triumphs and tribulations, ambitions and anxieties. Yet, as the king aged, the looming question of succession began to add darker hues to this elaborate piece. Like a game of knucklebones, the fortunes of Pyrrhus' lineage were precariously balanced, capable of swinging either way, and Pyrrhus, a player until the end, held his breath, awaiting the next roll.

In the annals of history, Pyrrhus of Epirus will be remembered not just for the vibrancy of his victories, but also for the subtle, shadow-dappled complexity of his twilight years. The king, the warrior, the philosopher – Pyrrhus was all these and more. As his sun started to set over the Epirote mountains, his legacy, much like the Homeric heroes of yore, seemed destined to echo through the corridors of time, long after the last light of his life had flickered out.

Yet, even in his twilight years, Pyrrhus remained unyielding, a testament to his indomitable spirit. He continued to cast his ambitious gaze towards horizons yet unconquered, his heart aflame with dreams of glory yet untasted. His ageing eyes, battle-hardened and world-weary, still held the fiery spark of a man who had lived life as though it was a grand epic, a man who, in the evening of his days, still embodied the spirit of the radiant dawn.

In his autumn, Pyrrhus was not a leaf to be swept away by the winds of time, but a majestic oak standing resolute, his roots firmly entrenched in the soils of his beloved Epirus, his branches reaching out to the vast expanses of the Hellenistic world. His later reign, though marked by the waning of his physical vitality, was a testament to the enduring vibrancy of his spirit and the indelible impact of his legacy.

In the twilight of Pyrrhus' reign, we see a king navigating the labyrinth of power with seasoned acuity, a warrior tempering his sword with wisdom, a philosopher contemplating the enigmatic riddle of fate. The tale of Pyrrhus is not one of relentless victory or crushing defeat, but of a man's unyielding perseverance in the face of time's relentless tide, a story of endurance and adaptation that resonates with timeless relevance.

Pyrrhus, in his later reign, mirrored the twilight itself - a blend of the departing day's realities and the approaching night's uncertainties, a time of reflection and anticipation, a time when the glimmers of the past meet the shadows of the future. His reign was an embodiment of the ceaseless flux of life, where triumph and adversity, strength and vulnerability, certainty and doubt dance in an eternal, intricate ballet.

Thus, in the twilight of his reign, Pyrrhus stood as a testament to the ebb and flow of power, the impermanence of mortal glory, and the undying quest for immortality through legacy. His is a tale etched in the sands of time, a saga that continues to whisper to us across the millennia, gently reminding us of our own ephemeral existence and the eternal rhythm of history.

CHAPTER 23:

The Fatal Rooftop: The Death of Pyrrhus

One of the most potent enigmas of human existence is the inevitability of death. Even for those who wear the mantle of power and command, who tower over the multitude like great statues hewn from stone, the final act must come. The sands in the hourglass run out; the stage darkens; the story concludes. Thus was the fate of Pyrrhus of Epirus, a man whose life was a stormy sea of victories and defeats, ambitions and disillusions, power and loss. His death, much like his life, was a compelling blend of the dramatic, the unexpected, and the tragically poetic.

The year was 272 BC, and the political landscape of Epirus and its environs was as volatile as a shimmering Greek summer, its days filled with the uncertain dance of alliances and conflicts. The indomitable Pyrrhus, still a potent force in this swirling vortex of power, had set his sights on the city of Argos, an ancient metropolis in the Peloponnese. This was a city that held more than just strategic value; it was a gem studded into the broad chest of Greece, a testament to the region's rich, layered history.

The accounts of Pyrrhus' death, like distant stars glimmering in the expanse of history, come to us shrouded in the mists of time. However, the story that emerges, pieced together from the scattered remnants of ancient chronicles, is as engaging as it is tragic. As Pyrrhus besieged Argos, he found himself embroiled in a labyrinth of local alliances, shifting loyalties, and strategic complexities. The city's formidable fortifications, its robust citizen-soldiers, and the intervention of his old adversary Antigonus II Gonatas of Macedonia made this no straightforward campaign.

The details of the final act of Pyrrhus' life unfurl like a Grecian tragedy. On that fateful day, the battle reached a fevered pitch within the city. As recounted by Plutarch, Pyrrhus had entered the city through one of its gates, guided by a local resident. However, in the chaotic dance of war, Pyrrhus and his forces were separated, and the king found himself in the heart of the city, amidst the tumultuous waves of conflict.

Here, amidst the narrow lanes of Argos, under the shadow of its grand structures, Pyrrhus, the lion of Epirus, met his end. Not on a vast battlefield arrayed with the spectacles of war, not in a grand duel with a rival king, but in the narrow, crowded alleyways of a besieged city. But even in death, Pyrrhus did not falter from his warrior's path. He was in the thick of the action, battling courageously despite the situation's dire nature.

The tableau of Pyrrhus' death resonates with an almost theatrical intensity. An old woman, looking down upon the violent spectacle from a rooftop, was moved by the sight of her son in mortal combat with

Pyrrhus. With a mother's desperate courage, she hurled a roof tile at Pyrrhus. The tile, guided by a combination of chance, destiny, or divine will, struck Pyrrhus on his head.

The blow, unexpectedly potent, dazed the seasoned warrior. Pyrrhus, disoriented, fell from his horse, an almost shocking sight in the midst of the melee. His guards tried to shield him, but in the confusion, an Argive soldier, Alcyoneus, recognised the dazed king. Rushing forward, Alcyoneus decapitated Pyrrhus, bringing a violent end to the life of the renowned warrior king.

Thus was the death of Pyrrhus - unexpected, dramatic, and brutally swift. A king who had defied fate numerous times, who had stood steadfast against the fiercest storms of conflict, met his end at the hands of an anonymous old woman and a local soldier. It was an ending that was starkly at odds with his life, filled with grand aspirations, mighty battles, and ruling a kingdom. Yet, perhaps there was a poignant poetry in this – the reminder that despite one's achievements and powers, death remains an inescapable reality, blind to status and indifferent to glory.

In death, Pyrrhus was stripped of his regalia, his majesty, his power. His decapitated body, devoid of the indomitable spirit it once housed, was a stark testament to the frailty of life. His head, the seat of his strategic acumen and kingly authority, was presented to Antigonus – a grim trophy signifying the end of a formidable adversary.

The news of Pyrrhus' death reverberated through the Hellenistic world like a thunderclap. The indomitable warrior king of Epirus, the formidable rival of Rome, the visionary who had dreamt of carving an empire, was no more. Epirus mourned the loss of its king, its protector, its most famous son. Across the Adriatic, Rome likely heaved a sigh of relief as their ambitious adversary had fallen. And in the wider Hellenistic world, the curtains had come down on one of the most dynamic sagas of their time.

In the chronicles of history, Pyrrhus of Epirus strides like a colossus, a warrior king whose life was a canvas of ambition, courage, and unyielding spirit. His death, dramatic as it was, only added another layer of intrigue to his larger-than-life persona. It was an event that sent ripples across the world he had known, shaping the fate of his kingdom and altering the trajectories of several others.

The death of Pyrrhus, much like his life, is a tale of unexpected turns, dramatic climaxes, and poignant realities. It's a sobering reminder of the indiscriminate nature of death, which doesn't distinguish between a king or a commoner, a warrior or a civilian. It's an end that illuminates the temporal, often fragile, nature of power and glory. For in the face of mortality, all earthly achievements dissolve into nothingness, and even the greatest amongst us must bow to this final, inexorable truth.

CHAPTER 24:

Successors and Failures: Epirus After Pyrrhus

The mighty oak had fallen. Pyrrhus, the relentless force that had driven the wheel of destiny in Epirus, lay cold and still. The echoes of his final battle, once a deafening roar, were now but a hushed whisper, weaving through the hills and valleys of Epirus. The tremors of his demise had left the kingdom bereft of its stalwart protector, its most vibrant son. Now, the land faced an uncertain future, its horizons cloaked in an eerie mist of ambiguity.

The death of Pyrrhus marked the cessation of a powerful current, one that had surged through the waters of Hellenistic politics with the ferocity of a thunderbolt. The ripples of this seismic shift were felt far beyond the rugged mountains of Epirus, across the Adriatic, through the corridors of power in Rome, and in the heartlands of Macedonia. But, nowhere was this change felt more acutely than in Epirus itself.

Epirus, the land that had shaped Pyrrhus, now had to confront a world without him. The kingdom had been swept up in his whirlwind of ambition, caught in the maelstrom of his dreams. His reign had been a wild tempest that tossed the kingdom between the peaks of glory and the troughs of disaster. His was an era defined by a relentless pursuit of power, a vision of Epirus as a formidable entity on the Hellenistic stage, a dream fueled by his indefatigable spirit. And with his sudden death, this tempest had passed, leaving behind a haunting stillness.

On the grand stage of Hellenistic politics, a vacuum was created. A king was dead, and a throne was vacant. Who would step into the breach? Who would grasp the scepter that Pyrrhus once wielded? The narrative that unfolded in the aftermath was a tale fraught with dynastic intrigues, dashed hopes, and the relentless march of time, washing away the vestiges of Pyrrhus' reign.

As the veil of the immediate mourning period lifted, the reality of the situation began to crystallize. The succession to the Epirote throne was far from clear, and multiple claimants vied for supremacy. At the forefront was Pyrrhus' son, Helenus. Young, untested, and thrown into the cauldron of power politics, Helenus found himself bearing the heavy mantle of kingship. He was to become a protagonist in a drama that he was ill-prepared for, a theatre of power, ambition, and treachery.

From the onset, Helenus was at the mercy of the tempestuous tide of events. Inheriting a kingdom that was still reeling from Pyrrhus' death, Helenus had a daunting task ahead. Pyrrhus had dominated the landscape of Epirus, a colossus whose shadow loomed over everything. Now, in his absence, the kingdom felt like a rudderless ship caught in a stormy sea.

The situation was exacerbated by external factors. Pyrrhus' ambitious ventures had earned him many adversaries, and with his death, these forces now viewed Epirus as a ripe target. The Kingdom of Macedon, under the resolute Antigonus II Gonatas, was a looming threat, and the promise of an alliance with this northern power, which had once served as a crucial counterweight in Pyrrhus' strategic balance, had been replaced by an unsettling tension. In the west, Rome, too, kept a watchful eye on the unfolding drama, its ambitions and apprehensions shaping its interactions with Epirus.

Under Helenus, Epirus plunged into a period of decline. Unable to fill his father's shoes, Helenus proved to be an ineffective ruler. His reign was marred by political instability, territorial losses, and increased Macedonian influence. The fervor and ambition that had marked Pyrrhus' rule was replaced with a languid melancholy, a pall of listlessness that seemed to grip Epirus.

It was in these troubled times that an intriguing character rose to the fore - Pyrrhus' other son, Alexander. Initially a peripheral figure, Alexander gradually began to assert himself, discontented with Helenus' rule. He saw in himself the true heir of Pyrrhus, the rightful bearer of his father's ambitions. In the simmering cauldron of Epirote politics, Alexander's ambitions were to add another potent ingredient.

The eventual clash between Helenus and Alexander was perhaps inevitable. A civil war ensued, plunging Epirus into further chaos. The Kingdom, which once under Pyrrhus had held its own against the might of Rome and Macedon, was now a battleground for a fraternal conflict. The city-states of Epirus, drawn into this internecine war, found themselves on opposing sides, further tearing the social fabric of the kingdom.

In this fraternal contest for power, there were no true winners. The civil war ended with Alexander seizing power, but at a great cost. The scars of this bitter conflict ran deep, and the kingdom was left in ruins. Alexander's reign, tarnished by the violence of his ascent and marked by his despotic tendencies, lacked the charisma and vision of Pyrrhus.

Epirus, under the successive reigns of Helenus and Alexander, was a pale shadow of its former self. The vibrancy and energy that Pyrrhus had brought to the kingdom were conspicuously absent. The grand dreams of an Adriatic empire, of standing toe-to-toe with the mighty forces of Rome and Macedon, had now faded into the realm of the past, replaced by an era of internal strife, external threats, and growing obscurity.

As the kingdom struggled to grapple with its stark reality, the ghost of Pyrrhus seemed to loom large. His legacy, once a beacon of Epirote power and glory, now seemed to cast a long, melancholic shadow over a kingdom in decline. The dreams of the philosopher-king were now but whispered legends, his victories treasured relics of a bygone era, his vision a distant mirage that had receded with his death.

In the labyrinthine corridors of time, the chapters following Pyrrhus' death bear testament to a stark reality – the unforgiving tide of history, the transient nature of power, and the inherent vulnerabilities of dynastic succession. They underscore the intricate tapestry of human ambition and failure, set against the relentless march of time. The rise and fall of Epirus post-Pyrrhus was not just a regional event. It was a human drama that played out on the grand stage of Hellenistic politics, its echoes resounding through the ages, long after the actors had exited the stage.

Epirus, the kingdom that had, under Pyrrhus, roared like a lion, seemed to whimper like a wounded animal in the aftermath. Yet, even in its decline, even in its moments of despair, the land retained an undeniable link to its golden era, a persistent memory of a king like no other. Even as the kingdom stumbled, the legacy of Pyrrhus remained etched into its identity, a testament to an indomitable spirit, an era of glory, and a dream that had once touched the very skies.

CHAPTER 25:

A Look at Pyrrhus Through the Eyes of Historians

The past, as they say, is another country. They do things differently there. This is an adage that the narrative historian understands only too well. The complex process of translating the sensibilities, expectations, and ambitions of bygone ages into the vocabulary of our present understanding is the historian's unending challenge.

The task becomes all the more daunting when the subject of inquiry is a figure like Pyrrhus of Epirus, a character who stands at the crossroads of myth and history, of heroism and hubris, of valour and vanity. Pyrrhus is a silhouette outlined by the fiery backdrop of the Hellenistic era, a shadow cast across centuries, compelling in its complexity, yet elusive in its essence.

The sands of historical analysis have shifted many times over the centuries, revealing and obscuring different facets of Pyrrhus' character and deeds. Like a seasoned archaeologist, the historian picks through the layered ruins of interpretation, examining the various artifacts of thought, the shards of analysis, to build a composite, a mosaic, of Pyrrhus, the man, and the monarch.

Our first historian's lens is the ancient one, through which we see Pyrrhus as a figure of legendary repute. Plutarch, writing a couple of centuries after Pyrrhus' death, cast him in the mold of a classical Greek hero. In his 'Parallel Lives', Plutarch traces the trajectory of Pyrrhus' life, portraying him as a valiant warrior king, a figure of pathos who came close to emulating the great Alexander, and yet, was ultimately felled by the inexorable wheel of fortune.

Yet, as Plutarch recounts his famous victories and his equally famous defeats, he presents Pyrrhus as a man swept up by his destiny, a player in the grand drama of history, rather than its scriptwriter. This Pyrrhus is a larger-than-life character, a figure of epic proportions, but with very little personal agency.

The next lens is the Roman one. Here, we find Pyrrhus reimagined as an antagonist, an existential threat to the nascent Roman Republic. Dionysius of Halicarnassus, another ancient historian, gave us a picture of Pyrrhus as a formidable adversary, who tested Rome's mettle like none before. However, in Dionysius' narrative, Pyrrhus' ultimate failure becomes a testament to Rome's indomitable spirit, turning Pyrrhus into a foil to highlight Rome's eventual ascendancy.

Flipping through the annals of medieval chronicles, we find Pyrrhus conspicuously absent, his story lost amidst the shadows of the Dark Ages. The vibrant tapestry of Hellenistic history had, by this time, been folded into the larger narratives of Rome's grandeur, leaving figures like Pyrrhus to languish in obscurity.

The dawn of the modern era, however, brought a new lens to bear upon the history of Pyrrhus. The intellectual ferment of the Renaissance sparked a renewed interest in the classical past, leading to a reappraisal of Hellenistic figures, Pyrrhus included.

In the works of historians like Barthold Georg Niebuhr and Johann Gustav Droysen, we find Pyrrhus depicted as a military genius, a master of strategy and tactics. His famed 'Pyrrhic victories' are presented not as imprudent follies, but as hard-won triumphs of martial prowess. But these historians also caution us about the dangers of overreach, showcasing Pyrrhus as a stark example of how unchecked ambition can lead to ruin.

The 20th century added yet another dimension to the historical assessment of Pyrrhus. In the shadow of the world wars, historians like Peter Green and N.G.L. Hammond have portrayed Pyrrhus as a victim of his era's tumultuous geopolitics. These historians saw in Pyrrhus a tragic figure, a man of immense potential thwarted by the cutthroat dynamics of a world in flux.

In their writings, Pyrrhus becomes a symbol of the futility of power, a poignant reminder that even the most valiant of kings can become mere pawns in the ruthless game of thrones. His life, in this interpretation, becomes a parable of the fleeting nature of glory, of the steep price one pays for ambition, and of the inherent fragility of human achievements.

The beauty of history lies in its plurality. It is a reflection in a shattered mirror, offering us a multitude of images, a spectrum of truths. In this case, each perspective, each lens, offers a unique vantage point into the life and times of Pyrrhus, enriching our understanding of the man and the monarch.

However, it is essential to remember that the process of historical analysis is akin to standing on the shores of a vast ocean, gazing into its unfathomable depths. We can perceive only the surface, discern only the broad patterns, while the intricate undercurrents remain hidden, inaccessible.

Pyrrhus, therefore, remains an enigma. Despite all our historical lenses and analytical tools, we can only approach a semblance of his true character, his motivations, his aspirations. We can sketch an outline, color it with assumptions and educated guesses, but the complete picture will always remain tantalizingly out of reach.

The silhouette of Pyrrhus, outlined against the fiery backdrop of the Hellenistic era, continues to draw us into its shadowy depths. It lures us with its complexity, its inscrutability, its tantalizing mix of heroism and hubris, valor, and vanity. It compels us to keep digging, to keep probing, to keep searching for the man behind the legend, the king beneath the crown, the human within the hero.

The sands of time may shift and obscure, reveal and conceal, but the pursuit of understanding never ends. And so, we continue to gaze into the past, to scrutinize the mirror of history, ever hopeful that we might catch a fleeting glimpse of Pyrrhus as he was, not as he has been imagined or interpreted to be. In that pursuit, we discover not just the enigmatic figure of Pyrrhus, but also the enduring allure of the past, and the infinite possibilities of historical understanding.

CHAPTER 26:

Myths, Legends, and Folklore of Pyrrhus

"History is not the soil in which memory grows but that which it grows in spite of" - this phrase, coined by John Bodnar, holds a special significance when contemplating the myths, legends, and folklore that have grown around Pyrrhus. This chapter is a discourse on the narrative spun by popular consciousness, separate from the austere evaluation of facts and circumstances.

In the embrace of collective memory, Pyrrhus is not a mere mortal king but a figure whose presence resonates beyond the measure of historical chronicles. He inhabits the ancient tales told by the hearth, the fables passed from generation to generation, the whispered stories that the night breeze carries across the centuries. Here, he is a god-born hero, an invincible warrior, a philosopher-king, an emblem of victory and defeat, and a symbol of glory and ruin.

It is a peculiar fact about human nature that we are often more comfortable with legends than with history. Legends are more forgiving; they allow us to project our hopes, our fears, our dreams, and our nightmares. They let us imagine a reality more exciting, more profound, and more resonant than the often-grim truths of history. Pyrrhus, in these tales, is no longer just an ancient king; he becomes an archetype, a symbol, a myth.

An enduring legend tells of Pyrrhus as a child of divine ancestry. As the tale goes, his mother, Phthia, was not impregnated by a mere mortal man but by the god of the silver bow, Apollo himself. This myth marks Pyrrhus as the descendant of Achilles, echoing the divine lineage of his legendary forefather. Apollo, the god of prophecy, imbued Pyrrhus with strategic insight, ensuring he would leave a mark on history. In the realm of myth, this imbued the young king with an aura of invincibility.

From the early days of his life in the rugged kingdom of Epirus to his last breath on the streets of Argos, the echo of Apollo was said to reverberate in his steps, his words, his actions. Apollo's gift was not just of strategic wisdom, but of charisma, of inspiration, of leadership. Pyrrhus was, in the eyes of the people, a god-touched king, his brilliance not just his own but a reflection of divine favour.

The myth of the Pyrrhic dance, an intricate display of military maneuvers performed with the grace and precision of a ballet, is another tale embedded in the folklore surrounding Pyrrhus. This dance was believed to have been inspired by Pyrrhus, who, as the story goes, saw in the harmonious motion of the celestial bodies a metaphor for the strategic movements of soldiers in battle. The Pyrrhic dance thus became a physical manifestation of Pyrrhus' philosophies of warfare and a testament to his military genius.

The tale of Pyrrhus' encounter with the Oracle of Delphi is another chapter of lore that survives. Seeking guidance before his fateful journey to Italy, Pyrrhus is said to have visited the Oracle. The prophecy was ambiguous, as Delphic prophecies often are: "I say, O Pyrrhus, that you, Achilles' kin, can win." It was a statement that could mean victory for either Rome or Pyrrhus. This story, in its subtle and poetic form, hints at the complexity of the king's Italian adventure.

Then there is the chilling folklore of Pyrrhus' death. In the land of Epirus, the elders still speak of an old woman's curse that sealed the fate of the great king. They say it was the spirit of a vengeful mother, mourning her son's death in the war, who guided that tile to Pyrrhus' head. The tale is a haunting testament to the cost of war, a poignant reminder that the mighty can be undone by the weak in the grand spectacle of fate.

Legends also tell of Pyrrhus' final battle with Rome, not in Italy, but in the underworld. They say that every time Rome teetered on the edge of disaster, Pyrrhus would rise from the shadows, his bronze armor gleaming, his ashen spear poised to strike. He would lead the spirits of those who had fallen against Rome, their spectral army a symbol of defiance and resilience. Pyrrhus, in death as in life, was a nemesis that Rome could not forget.

Each of these stories, in its own way, illuminates a different facet of Pyrrhus' persona. They may not adhere to the rigorous scrutiny of history, but they capture the essence of the man and the king in a way that dry facts and chronicles can never hope to. Through these myths and legends, Pyrrhus becomes more than a character in a history book; he becomes a part of the cultural consciousness, a figure that transcends the barrier of time.

Whether it was the tale of his divine birth, his inspired dance, his cryptic oracle, his haunting death, or his eternal battle against Rome, these narratives persist because they tap into something primal, something universal. They transform the king from Epirus into a figure of timeless resonance.

The legends of Pyrrhus are mirrors held up to human nature, reflecting our desires, our anxieties, our dreams, and our fears. These stories may not be accurate in the strictest historical sense, but they carry their truth, a truth that is more profound, more poignant, more human. And, in the end, isn't that what all great stories strive for? Isn't that why we still, after more than two millennia, speak of Pyrrhus of Epirus?

CHAPTER 27:

The Legacy of Pyrrhus in Modern Culture

As the first rays of dawn strike the jagged Acropolis, it is time to ask: what are the echoes of Pyrrhus in our contemporary world? We know him well by now. Our journey through the life of this audacious king has entailed not just a chronological trudge through time, but a creative exploration, an unlocking of doors into past events and characters, a way of seeing our world with new eyes. We have found Pyrrhus the man, warrior, king, and philosopher, at the helm of fierce battles, caught in political intrigues, pacing palace corridors deep in thought, even peering at the heavens in search of divine guidance. But let us consider this man and his legacy as it echoes across the ages to our own times.

In the modern world, Pyrrhus remains a potent symbol of both greatness and futility. It is a stark, jarring juxtaposition, certainly, but one that we can hear echoed in the musings of scholars, in the pages of literature, and in the still, silent frames of film. He is hailed as a military genius whose innovative tactics have been studied in war academies and whose strategic acumen has informed some of the most critical decisions of world leaders. His very name has etched itself into the vernacular, spawning the term

'Pyrrhic victory,' and embedding itself into our collective consciousness. Yet, beyond the battlefield and the lexicon, Pyrrhus's legacy thrives, telling tales of audacious ambition and its cost, of noble intentions that get mired in their own execution.

Literature, the ripest field for ideas and allegories to flourish, has been an especially welcoming home for Pyrrhus. As a character or symbol, he looms large, as vivid as his contemporaries would have perceived him, a man who once bestrode the world like a colossus, only to see his dreams turn to ashes. The grand tapestry of literature, woven from the threads of countless narratives and insights, gives Pyrrhus his rightful place. He is found in the pages of books and plays, offering us a way to understand human ambition, to make sense of the chaotic tangle of desires and actions that drive us, to question the very nature of success and failure.

One such example is Herman Melville's novella, 'Billy Budd, Sailor'. Melville's use of the term 'Pyrrhic victory' is particularly poignant, as it becomes a prism through which we view the complex interplay between power, ethics, and tragic inevitability. And in the realm of theatre, Robert Bolt's 'Man for All Seasons' has Sir Thomas More referring to a Pyrrhic victory, evoking the inevitable costs of moral and political compromises.

In film, Pyrrhus becomes both myth and man. The 1962 Italian epic, 'Warrior of Epirus', presented a romanticized version of Pyrrhus, full of honor, ambition, and tragedy. This figure, larger than life, marched across the silver screen with such vibrancy that it was as if the very spirit of ancient Epirus had come to life in post-war Italy. The film, a box-office success, rekindled interest in the figure of Pyrrhus, and inspired a generation of filmmakers and screenwriters to explore the fertile ground of ancient history. More recent depictions, like 'Empire of the Sun,' a 2022 British biographical drama, cast a more nuanced gaze at Pyrrhus, focusing as much on his philosophical insights and political acumen as his martial prowess.

The 21st century has also seen Pyrrhus's life explored in other creative mediums. Graphic novels like 'Tides of Fortune: Pyrrhus of Epirus' have brought his story to younger audiences with evocative illustrations and engaging narratives. Video games like the 'Total War' series allow players to assume the role of Pyrrhus and command his armies in the Italian peninsula and beyond, grappling with the same strategic dilemmas the king himself once faced.

Pyrrhus's legacy has also found its way into modern scholarly debates, his life serving as a case study in the paradoxes of power and ambition. His military innovations are regularly studied in war colleges and strategic institutes around the world. His philosophy of kingship and statecraft find themselves explored in political science and philosophy departments. Even business schools, ever on the hunt for historical analogies to illuminate modern challenges, turn to Pyrrhus's story, debating the wisdom and costs of his expansive ambitions.

The resonance of Pyrrhus in modern culture, however, goes beyond academic institutions, creative mediums, or even popular discourse. The very narratives we construct to make sense of our world often carry a touch of Pyrrhus. The ambitious entrepreneur who sacrifices personal life for business success, the athlete who suffers debilitating injuries for a moment of glory, the statesman who compromises core principles for political gains - all are versions of Pyrrhic victories, reminding us that success is not always what it seems, that victory can come at a devastating cost.

As we peel back the layers of his life, as we gaze at the frescoes of history that bear his likeness, we see Pyrrhus, not just as a figure of antiquity, but a vibrant part of our collective cultural heritage. His legacy, etched in the annals of time and the rhythm of language, reminds us of the eternal human saga, of our ceaseless striving for glory and our enduring struggle with ambition. As we journey through our lives in the shadow of this bygone king, let us remember Pyrrhus not just as a relic of the past but as a mirror held up to our times. A mirror that reflects our victories and defeats, our dreams and disillusionments, and the fragile human condition that binds us all. And as we continue to build upon the edifice of human civilization, let us be mindful of the Pyrrhic victories we court, and remember that there is always a price to be paid, always a dream that can turn to dust.

CHAPTER 28:

Pyrrhus and Rome: A Relationship Revisited

The hourglass, with its tiny grains of sand falling from one glass chamber to another, marks not only the relentless passing of time but also a ceaseless flow of historical forces and personalities, constantly shaping and reshaping one another. On the shifting sands of antiquity, two such forces, Pyrrhus of Epirus and the nascent might of Rome, found themselves intertwined, creating a relationship as intriguing as it was impactful. Their collision left an indelible mark on the historical narrative, shaping the destinies of both entities, and causing ripples that reached far beyond the realm of the ancients. This chapter is an attempt to revisit this complex relationship, to explore its depths and understand its profound significance.

Our narrative begins with Rome, a burgeoning power growing from a humble city-state into a regional power. Like a hungry beast, it spread its wings, consuming the tribes and cities of Italy into its expanding territorial belly. The landscape of Italy was being redrawn, and the Italian people were caught in a whirlwind of rapid political change.

Into this turbulent theatre came Pyrrhus of Epirus, a king, a warrior, a philosopher. It was a call for aid from

Tarentum, a city threatened by Rome's territorial hunger, which drew Pyrrhus from his Epirote homeland and cast him onto the Italian stage. Yet, this encounter was not simply a momentary clash of arms, but a profound meeting of cultures and philosophies, of two different approaches to power and rule. It was a struggle between two visions of empire: Rome, with its focus on statecraft and the rule of law, and Pyrrhus, who believed in the power of personal leadership and the guiding light of philosophy.

Pyrrhus, armed with the traditional Hellenistic idea of the warrior king, led his forces personally into the heat of battle. In this, he mirrored the heroes of Homeric epics, living by a chivalric code of personal bravery and martial excellence. Rome, on the other hand, had already begun to weave the fabric of institutional governance, setting the foundation for what would eventually become the Roman bureaucratic machine. Where Pyrrhus led his men from the front, the Romans invested authority in the Senate and the Consuls, maintaining a delicate balance of power within its political sphere.

The battlefield exploits between Pyrrhus and Rome have been explored in detail, and there is little need for repetition here. However, it is worth considering the legacy of their conflict, especially the concept of a Pyrrhic victory. Despite Pyrrhus' tactical successes, the sheer cost of his victories, in terms of men and materiel, rendered them hollow. Yet, in this paradoxical success lay a deeper truth, a truth that would reveal itself more fully as Rome expanded its domains across the ancient world.

Pyrrhus was not merely a tactical genius on the battlefield; he was a shrewd observer of politics and power dynamics. He witnessed Rome's rapid growth, its systemic political structure, and the fierce discipline of its legions. He would have perceived the Roman ethos: duty, order, and a relentless drive for expansion. One can imagine Pyrrhus, amidst the carnage of the battlefield, glimpsing the future of Rome, seeing in it a force that would ultimately consume the Hellenistic world.

Conversely, Rome, too, had lessons to learn from Pyrrhus. The very term 'Pyrrhic victory', coined from their encounters, would have left a lasting impression on the Roman psyche. They would have seen the devastating costs of military hubris and the wisdom in avoiding wasteful victories. Furthermore, in Pyrrhus, the Romans encountered a leader who was not merely a king but a philosopher and a scholar, qualities they would have admired and, perhaps, sought to emulate in their own leaders.

While it is true that Pyrrhus ultimately departed Italy, failing to halt the march of Rome, it is equally true that the encounter left a lasting impact on both parties. For Pyrrhus, it represented a glimpse of the future, a vision of the rising power of Rome. It was an experience that likely influenced his subsequent decisions, shaping his policy and philosophy in ways that, perhaps, we can only begin to comprehend. For Rome, the encounter with Pyrrhus served as a testament to the power of individual leadership and the dangers of costly victories, lessons that would echo through their history.

As we revisit the relationship between Pyrrhus and Rome, we find a nuanced tapestry of interplay and influence. Both Rome and Pyrrhus left indelible marks on each other, shaping each other's history and future. The relationship, thus, was not merely of enemies on a battlefield, but of mutual influencers, leaving lasting imprints on the sands of time.

So, let the hourglass flip again, for we have revisited a significant chapter of history. As the grains of sand continue to fall, so too do the chapters of history continue to unfold, each subtly shaped by the ones that came before it. The sands of Pyrrhus and Rome have fallen, yet their imprints remain, a testament to their timeless dance, forever etched in the annals of history.

CHAPTER 29:

The Lessons of Pyrrhus

The life of Pyrrhus of Epirus is the proverbial well that never runs dry – it is a perennial source of lessons, questions, and endless fascination. Pyrrhus, the proverbial David facing the imperial Goliaths of his time, never ceased in his quest to carve his own destiny amidst a world stage fraught with political intrigue, complex relationships, and continuous warfare. His is a tale of ambition, cunning, courage, and above all, an unquenchable thirst for power. The past, after all, is not merely a monolithic entity – it is a living, breathing entity, eternally altering and shaping itself under the scrutinizing lens of human examination.

The story of Pyrrhus compels us to engage with such questions and reflects upon our own values, actions, and decisions. We must ask ourselves, what is the measure of a man's life? Is it his deeds or the legacy he leaves behind? Pyrrhus, in his glory and failures, offers us a complex answer, one filled with nuances, paradoxes, and much room for contemplation.

Often, history doesn't simply celebrate the victorious; it also pays heed to those who, though they may have faltered, displayed unparalleled determination and resilience. Pyrrhus was indeed a King, a Warrior, and a Philosopher, but more importantly, he was a testament to human spirit and will. His life, a beacon of hope in a sea of adversity, provides us with multiple lenses to dissect and learn from.

One of the most compelling lessons emanates from Pyrrhus' sheer tenacity. His perseverance in the face of adversity, his indomitable spirit in the wake of seemingly insurmountable obstacles, paint the picture of a man who refused to accept defeat. History is laden with figures who bowed before the inevitability of their circumstances. Pyrrhus, however, stood tall, navigating the stormy seas of his era with a relentless pursuit of his dreams. His life serves as a testament to the power of resilience and determination.

Yet, in examining Pyrrhus' resilience, we are also confronted with the precarious balance between ambition and hubris. Pyrrhus' relentless pursuit of glory brought him as many tragedies as it did triumphs. As we turn the pages of his life, we can't help but wonder if Pyrrhus was aware of the invisible line he crossed, from unyielding ambition into the realm of destructive hubris. His life becomes a poignant lesson on the potency of ambition, and the potential self-destruction that can ensue when it becomes unbridled.

The strategic brilliance of Pyrrhus is another crucial aspect of his life that offers insights into the art of leadership and the conduct of war. Pyrrhus' victories against Rome, despite the exorbitant cost that led to the coining of the term 'Pyrrhic victory', were due in large part to his understanding of battlefield tactics, his innovative use of elephants, and his ability to motivate his troops. These victories were not just a testament to his military genius, but also an exemplification of the power of innovative thinking and effective leadership.

However, the shadows of his losses loom large. Pyrrhus, despite his military acumen, found himself in a series of conflicts that gradually eroded his power and influence. His incessant campaigns, one after another, bled his kingdom dry and left him increasingly isolated. It was not the want of bravery or strategy that brought Pyrrhus low, but rather, the inability to acknowledge when to stop. This part of Pyrrhus' life provides a cautionary tale about the dangers of overextension and the importance of knowing one's limits.

When we delve into the philosophical mind of Pyrrhus, we encounter a king who aspired to more than just military triumphs. Pyrrhus, the philosopher-king, yearned for a harmonious state, a realm that was as prosperous in its culture and intellect as it was formidable in war. Pyrrhus' relationship with his subjects, his patronage of arts and sciences, and his desire for enlightened rule, albeit punctuated with instances of cruelty, offer profound lessons on the nature of effective governance and the quest for a balanced society.

But the philosophy of Pyrrhus, like the man himself, is layered with contradictions. His vision of a prosperous, enlightened realm stood in stark contrast to his pursuit of incessant warfare and territorial conquest. The philosopher in Pyrrhus grappled with the warrior, creating a dichotomy that defined his rule and inevitably contributed to his downfall. This incongruity in Pyrrhus' life imparts the lesson that actions, no matter how grand the intent, must align with the moral and philosophical beliefs one espouses.

Pyrrhus' life is not merely a historical account to be studied; it is a narrative brimming with lessons, a narrative that forces us to confront our own beliefs, our understanding of success, ambition, and moral values. It teaches us about the consequences of hubris, the power of innovation, and the crucial importance of balance in leadership. It makes us wonder about the potential within each of us and the heights to which we could ascend—or the depths to which we could fall—depending on the paths we choose. In essence, the story of Pyrrhus isn't just about an ambitious king from Epirus. It is a mirror reflecting the triumphs, failures, hopes, and fears inherent in the human condition.

Despite his ultimate downfall, Pyrrhus remains one of history's most intriguing figures. His tale invites us to embark on a journey of introspection, prompting us to learn from the past, live in the present, and aspire for a better future. The enigmatic King of Epirus, in his victories and his losses, in his brilliance and his flaws, in his moments of both wisdom and folly, offers a canvas of human nature in all its complexity. His life whispers a multitude of lessons that echo through the corridors of time, making Pyrrhus of Epirus a figure not just of history, but also of immense, timeless significance.

CHAPTER 30:

The Hourglass of Pyrrhus

As we descend into the final act of our chronicle, the echo of Pyrrhus's footsteps growing faint in the corridors of time, we come face to face with a question: How do we perceive the life of a man once steeped in power and authority, who dared to challenge the destinies of nations, and who now rests in the forgotten periphery of history?

The Hourglass of Pyrrhus. Time, a constant flux, moving relentlessly like grains of sand in an hourglass, has placed him within a context, both elevating and diminishing his deeds in equal measures. Each tick and tock of the cosmic clock has bestowed upon Pyrrhus a certain timelessness and an eternity of obscurity, making him a name remembered, yet not quite recalled.

Every life tells a story, and the essence of a story lies not in the outcome but in the journey. And what a journey it was for the King of Epirus, who lived life on the edge of a sword, scribed history with the tip of a spear, and left an indelible mark on the sands of time.

History, much like a flowing river, constantly reshapes the landscape, shifting from one course to another, creating and destroying in equal measures. To understand the significance of Pyrrhus, we must see him as a river's tumultuous current, as a force shaping the geopolitical terrain of his time, as a monument to the allure of ambition, and the inevitability of transience.

In the endless meandering narrative of human civilization, Pyrrhus serves as a reminder that the rise and fall of great men and their empires is a cyclical dance to the rhythm of time. His life, brimming with triumphs and failures, victories, and defeats, provides a panoramic view of the dance between ambition and destiny, power and fallibility.

The narrative of Pyrrhus speaks not just of a man's rise from obscurity to the zenith of power, but also of the inherent ephemerality of worldly glory. Pyrrhus' journey, much like that of countless others before and after him, serves to underscore the age-old adage - sic transit gloria mundi - thus passes the glory of the world.

But to see Pyrrhus merely as a symbol of fleeting glory would be an oversimplification, a disservice to the complexity of his life and times. Beneath the surface of his military exploits, we find a man deeply entrenched in the philosophical traditions of his time, grappling with questions of morality, justice, and duty.

Pyrrhus, the philosopher king, imbued his reign with an enlightened vision, a blend of practical governance and philosophical idealism. His ideals, while not always perfectly manifested, provided an anchor, a guiding light in the tempest of his turbulent reign.

Pyrrhus was not a mere puppet in the theatre of history. He was a puppeteer, a strategist manipulating the strings of power, influencing the course of events. He was the sculptor and the sculpture, simultaneously shaping and being shaped by the tumultuous world around him.

The sands of time may have weathered the statue of Pyrrhus, fading the intricate details, mellowing the sharp contours. But the statue stands, nonetheless, a testament to the King of Epirus who dared to gaze upon the world, not as a passive observer, but as an active participant, a changer of fates and shifter of paradigms.

His impact may not have changed the world in the way Alexander the Great's did, but it was significant in its own right. His defiance of Rome, his audacity in challenging the emerging superpower, sparked the resilient flame of resistance, illuminating the stage for the epic Punic Wars that were to follow.

And even in death, Pyrrhus became a beacon, a beacon that threw a penetrating light on the brutal realities of the Hellenistic world, revealing the fragility of alliances, the fickleness of fortune, and the insatiable hunger for power. His untimely demise echoed the tragic truth - the dance with destiny could often end in an unexpected and abrupt whirl, leaving a void and a tale of what could have been.

So, as we reach the end of our journey, we find ourselves standing at the crossroads of history, gazing back at the footprints left by Pyrrhus. His life, filled with dizzying highs and devastating lows, paints a picture of a man who embraced his destiny, who dared to dream, to aspire, to achieve.

The hourglass of Pyrrhus, with its relentless ebb and flow, serves as a poignant metaphor for the inescapable cycle of life and history. Just as the sands slip from one chamber to another, so too did Pyrrhus transition from king to exile, conqueror to fallen hero, mortal to legend. The grains of sand in the hourglass, once part of a magnificent spectacle, now lie silent and still - a poignant testament to the transient yet timeless saga of Pyrrhus of Epirus.

In this hourglass, we find not only the encapsulation of a single life but also the microcosm of the human narrative - of ambition and downfall, power and loss, courage and vulnerability. It is a narrative of the dance with destiny and the enduring allure of the dreams of glory - a narrative that continues to reverberate through the corridors of history, a tale as timeless as the man himself.

As the echo of Pyrrhus's footsteps fade into the annals of history, his legacy, much like the timeless grains in the hourglass, remains - etched in the memories of those who dared to dream, to conquer, to defy. The tale of Pyrrhus of Epirus, in its essence, remains a timeless narrative of human resilience, ambition, and the impermanence of power. It serves as a timeless reflection on the enduring human saga - a saga of ambitions unfettered, dreams realized and shattered, and life, in all its glory and despair.

In the grand theatre of history, Pyrrhus stands not merely as a character but as a testament to the human spirit's indomitable courage and resolve. His tale, resounding through the epochs, reminds us of the fleeting nature of power and the timeless value of wisdom. The sands of time may run their course, kingdoms may rise and fall, but the tale of a King, a Warrior, and a Philosopher of Ancient Greece endures, an eternal narrative in the Hourglass of Pyrrhus.

Your Voice, Our Beacon

Dear Reader,

If you have reached this point, you have braved the wilds of Epirus with us, walked the marble halls of ancient courts, heard the clashing of iron on the battlefields, and eavesdropped on the quiet murmur of philosophical musings. You, my companion on this journey, have breathed life into Pyrrhus's story, giving it voice in our shared world. Thank you for that.

Now that you've walked in Pyrrhus' sandals, heard the cries of his armies, felt the joy of his triumphs, and the sting of his defeats, it's time for us to listen to you. Your experience, your interpretation, your feelings matter - after all, what is a story if not a shared understanding between the teller and the listener?

And so, we humbly ask you, would you share your thoughts?

Amazon, our marketplace of ideas, is a perfect place for this dialogue. Your review, a guiding light in the vast ocean of books, could lead another reader to the shores of Epirus, to the story we've shared. It's not about stars or rankings; it's about sharing your journey through Pyrrhus' life, about finding like-minded companions who also wish to travel back in time and explore the uncharted territories of the human heart and mind.

Yes, your review is that important! A few sentences, some heartfelt thoughts, can illuminate the way for others. It can make the difference between our book finding a home on another reader's nightstand, or being lost in the annals of countless tales.

As an author, I can attest - nothing is more gratifying than knowing that our work has found resonance with a reader. Your review gives us that affirmation. It provides a connection, a spark, that fuels our creative efforts and ignites our passion to keep crafting stories that entertain, inform, and inspire.

So, if you've been moved, challenged or even simply entertained by Pyrrhus' story, please consider leaving a review. Share your own insights, your revelations, or just how this story made you feel. Your words can weave into this historical tapestry we've tried to create, adding depth and vibrancy to the narrative.

By writing a review, you become a part of the book's journey, its narrative. You add to Pyrrhus' legacy, and to the ongoing discourse about our past, our present, and our shared humanity.

So, pull up a seat at the table of conversation, and let us know your thoughts. Remember, every voice counts in the grand symphony of shared knowledge and wisdom. And we eagerly await to hear yours.

As we close this chapter and turn the page, know that our shared journey through Pyrrhus' life doesn't end here. It lives on in our thoughts, our conversations, and in the insights we carry with us.

We look forward to hearing from you. And once again, thank you for taking this journey with us.

Printed in Great Britain
by Amazon